ASADA

BRICIA LOPEZ

WITH
JAVIER CABRAL

THE ART OF MEXICAN-STYLE GRILLING

Abrams
New York

To Eduardo and Augustina, by far
the two greatest things I've ever created

INTRODUCTION

Carne asada
is not just a taco.

In millions of backyards across Southern California,
an asada represents more than just meat. It means
family, friends, memories, great music, cold drinks,
good times, and the community you've built—all
centered on the promise of juicy grilled meat and all
the fixings that remind you of your upbringing. The
smell of asada is an invisible cloud of joy that forever
lingers around the streets of Los Angeles. In a city
like L.A., where the taco is a way of life, backyard
asada culture is as respected as church on Sundays.
Inviting someone to your carne asada is a gesture of
love, respect, generosity, and friendship. It's a way
of welcoming you and feeding you like family. At its
most essential, all you really need for a proper carne
asada is some meat, tortillas, and salsa. But a true
carne asada is only as good as you prepare it to be.
Every family has their own secret carne asada recipe
or their go-to *carnicería* (meat market) that they will
defend and stay loyal to for having the best marinated
beef, pork, and chicken.

An asada can be as intimate or as big as you'd like it
to be. You don't need to celebrate anything but life
to gather loved ones and throw an asada, though a
birthday asada is always my favorite.

I'll never forget hosting my first asada as an adult in
my own home. It was not only a rite of passage but one
of the first times in my life I felt like a real adult. I was
nervous my marinades wouldn't hold up, that I would
run out of food, that my mom would find my salsas
bland, and that my tortillas would burn before they hit
the table.

Things have changed quite a bit since then.
Allow me to walk you through what an asada looks
like in my house. An asada almost always begins with
a short guest list that will eventually double in size.
I begin preparations the night before, by marinating
the meat, soaking beans, and making at the very least
two to three different salsas. With hands reeking of
garlic and onion, no matter how many times I try to
wash it away, I call it a night and try to get as much
rest as possible. The next day I'll wake up with a text

9

from my sister saying her boyfriend's brother and two friends are in town. Yes, they are also coming to the asada, and I have the startling realization that I won't have enough time to marinate extra meat. This is when trusting your local Mexican grocery store is important. I roll out of bed, shower, and put on my matching sweatpant set, and before heading out, I put a large pot of beans on the stove to cook.

I then drive to my dearest local Mexican grocery store and grab a couple of pounds of marinated pollo asado and *arrachera* (skirt steak). I take this time to also grab a bag of chicharrónes, extra cheeses, and any last-minute pantry items we need. I get home to receive another text, this time from my brother, letting me know he too will be rolling through with a couple of extra homies. I am thankful I grabbed that extra pound of marinated arrachera. I quickly check on my beans; they are perfect. I get started on my red rice, a dish only reserved for days like these. It's a staple at every asada. I work on my nopalito salad, snack on store-bought chips and salsa, and begin assembling my fruit salad, and the chicharrónes and cheese board, knowing I'll have a few guests trickling in any minute.

An asada's start time is more a "suggested time of arrival," and everyone has their preconceived notion on when an asada should begin. I like to tell people two P.M. Again, this is a suggested time. Most will begin trickling in between three P.M. and as late as six. Only time will tell when the day is over. The first batch of guests to arrive will always have my personally marinated pieces of meat; this is the reward for being "on time" to the asada. My youngest sister is usually the first to arrive. I like to believe it's because she doesn't have any kids, but then again, people who arrive on time to an asada are a species of their own. She quickly claims a chair or two by placing her bag or some sort of extra layer of clothing on them. Though an asada almost always takes part in an outdoor setting, in my house, it starts in my kitchen. I'm never ready for the first guest. They are the ones who see a glimpse of the storm before the calm. I am either reheating my beans, finishing my spread of salsas, frantically remembering to make an agua fresca for the kids, or reminding my

husband about the melting ice bags that need to get into the cooler. The grill doesn't get started until an hour after the first guest has arrived.

A classic night full of carne asada with friends and family goes like this: A random *tío* (uncle) or maybe even your father or brother drinks way too much and starts to either fall asleep or reminisce about the days when he was younger and how different things were; a primo and a friend will disappear for a few minutes to "go for a walk" and return extra giggly and hungry; your niece or nephew will be asleep in the most uncomfortable position in a chair somewhere right in front of the thumping speaker, and only real ones will stay extra late to help you clean up before they go home.

A well-prepared asada gathering can be the difference between enjoying your own party or feeling like it was just an extra day of work. The responsibility of being an asada grill master for the day comes with great privilege, and a cold beer to get you through it all. Fortunately for everyone, backyard-style carne asada is extremely forgiving. If we are being honest, many of us love and actually prefer the pieces of carne that are well beyond "well-done." Burned, even, or what we Mexicans like to refer to as *bien doradito* ("extra crispy"). Hosting and making carne asada gets easier and more streamlined the more you do it. When you are first starting out, it's OK to run out of meat. It happens. Next time, you will now know how much to buy per person, and even then you may mess up. The skill of knowing how much food to prepare is something you will master through years of experience.

You will eventually start to develop a system and know how long it takes to get the fire started, how late your guests usually are, and how to achieve a foolproof tortilla-to-person ratio along with that meat-per-person ratio. But if you take one thing from this book, it is this: Throwing a carne asada is an act of love.

And yes, you are invited to the asada.

A Brief History
of Asada Culture

Carne asada as sustenance goes back to the first time humans controlled fire and placed a piece of hunted meat over it, about a million years ago or so. The first microscopic traces of wood ash go back that long. Carne asada as a pastime in Mexico took off in the 1950s, specifically in the northern and northeastern regions of Sonora and Nuevo León. Spanish Jesuit colonizers settled in these regions in the 1530s. This early adoption of meat-eating, in a country that primarily consumed beans and insects for protein before the Spanish conquest, allowed Sonora and Nuevo León to develop thriving cattle industries and consistent access to the freshest and best beef in the country.

When immigrants from Mexico started to come to the United States in the 1900s, they brought along their love of grilled carne asada. The earliest mention of a carnicería in the United States in print publications goes back to 1930. Over the decades, carnicerías popped up around the country, especially in the places many Mexican immigrants called home, like Los Angeles, Chicago, and the Bay Area. By the seventies, you started to see thin marinated skirt—flap meat—steaks in butcher cases ready to be grilled at home. Since then, it has become the go-to meal to celebrate birthdays, life milestones, or just another weekend.

It wasn't until recently that true carne asada started to become a thing in taco culture, thanks to the growth of taquerías in Los Angeles doing Tijuana-style tacos. This T.J. taco style brought mesquite-grilled juicy asada to the masses and created a new standard: If you don't see smoke, it's not true carne asada. At home, backyard carne asadas are still the go-to celebratory meal for many Mexican families of all generations and classes.

The Asada Pantry

Those of us who live in major cities are fortunate to never be too far away from a well-stocked Mexican supermarket. In many cities, there are still many small Mexican corner tienditas where you can also find a lot of the staples needed for an asada. Sometimes, a small Mexican market may have better quality or certain harder-to-find ingredients. I've gone to a supermarket for some items and a tiendita for other things. You can find any dried chile featured in this book and so many more obscure ones to experiment with online. If looking in a non-Mexican supermarket, the dried chiles are usually in the spice section.

Here is how to maneuver your way through all the aisles.

Chiles

The number one rule when working with dried chiles is to remember to not touch your eyes for a couple of hours after handling them. The capsaicin of both dried and fresh chiles has a tendency to stay on your fingertips no matter how many times you wash your hands. To stay one step ahead of the chiles, you can always use disposable gloves when working with them, fresh and dried.

ANAHEIM: This fresh green chile begs to be fire-roasted. It is big enough to stuff, meaty enough to slice to use like a bell pepper, and can be mashed or blended to make a chunky salsa. Anaheims tend to be on the mild side. The seeds can be big, so make sure to remove them before roasting.

CASCABEL: This Christmas tree ornament–shaped round chile gets its name for the rattling noise it makes when you shake one and hears the seeds bouncing around inside. Cascabel means "rattle." Its flavor is woodsy, bright, and nuttier than other chiles.

CHILE DE ÁRBOL: Whenever you need a blast of quick and peppery heat to any salsa, dried chiles de árbol are there for you. Add one by one until the desired spiciness is reached.

CHILES GÜEROS: In the American southwest, these chiles used to be known as the "Santa Fe Grande." They are an excellent fresh chile for beginners because they are on the sweet and mild side, but still pack that fresh chile flavor, especially when charred. They are a little fatter than a jalapeño. Look for chiles that have a thick, juicy-looking skin.

CHIPOTLE: Chipotle is the most popular dried chile because it made the crossover to the American mainstream and because it is sold pre-hydrated in a can of delicious adobo. Just open a can and you're ready to go. Chipotle's flavor is universally beloved for its smokey and fruity flavor with a heat that can be easily controlled.

DRIED GUAJILLO AND GUAJILLO POWDER: Guajillo is a dried chile with medium-level heat. It has a nice balance of fruity and smoky flavors. While Mexican cooking usually relies on rehydrating whole dried chiles for salsas and sauces, we use it in its dried ground form when seasoning a dry rub.

DRIED PASILLA AND ANCHO POWDER: Pasilla is the dried version of poblanos; it is also known as a chile negro. It is the fruitiest of the dried chiles and packs in the flavor without delivering much heat. Dried ancho chile is potent and goes a long way in a rub.

MORITA CHILE: If you prefer a spicier, less-smokey, and even fruitier alternative to chipotle, then morita chile is for you. It is also a jalapeño, but is ripened until red, so its flavor is spicier and more intense than chipotle. It can be substituted in equal parts with chipotle.

POBLANOS: This is the workhorse of Mexico's chiles for its ability to be served either as a main course when roasted and stuffed with cheese or eaten like a vegetable when grilled and cut into thick strips. Its meaty texture is incredibly satisfying. While most poblanos are not spicy, you may get one every once in a while that is incredibly fiery. Look for bulb-shaped chiles that do not have wrinkly edges, as wrinkles indicate that they are not fresh.

SERRANOS AND JALAPEÑOS: These two fresh chiles are the most popular varieties to use in the salsas you will find in a carne asada. They can be used interchangeably in recipes and taste great both in their raw and charred state. We prefer serranos for their higher level of heat and grassier flavor. Look for serranos that are firm, plump, and free of wrinkles.

Citrus

MEXICAN KEY LIMES: This is the most indispensable ingredient in the universe of Mexican food but in a carne asada, key limes make virtually anything taste better. These smaller, golf ball–shaped limes have a more tropical flavor without much bitterness, so we prefer these when they are available. Look for limes with no brown leathery splotches, which are an indicator that they are on their way out and taste unpleasantly oxidized. Always make sure to offer sliced limes at a carne asada spread so that your guests can squeeze away at their hearts' content.

ORANGE: Orange juice is unmatched in a marinade because of its high acid content, which has the ability to tenderize the meat while adding a subtle sweetness to it at the same time. Use juice from fresh oranges when in season.

Fresh Herbs

CILANTRO: Bright and lemony, and to a certain percentage of the population soapy, even, cilantro is a staple in carne asadas. In fact, many times it is the only green available to provide a color and flavor contrast. It deserves a permanent spot on your weekly grocery list because it is so versatile as a garnish for tacos, rice, and salsas. Look for cilantro bunches with firm stems and no yellow leaves.

EPAZOTE: A little of this pungent herb goes a long way. It is mostly used in central and southern Mexico and is beloved for its earthy and potent herbaceous flavor. It is also miraculous because it aids in the digestion of beans. Look for epazote that has a strong smell and firm stems. Unfortunately, dried epazote won't do for most applications where fresh epazote is called for, but you can use fresh cilantro in a pinch.

MINT: When all else fails, add a little mint. It works equally well in savory and sweet dishes, and always livens things up when used as a garnish.

PARSLEY: Parsley has a place in carne asadas for its sharp and peppery flavor. We use it in marinades and serve it with cheese. We always buy flat-leaf parsley, also known as "Italian," because its flavor is a little stronger than that of its curly counterpart.

Spices

CUMIN: Cumin is a great way to build flavor in a dish. Whether in a marinade or as a rub, its bold flavor is unmistakable at first bite.

GARLIC POWDER: Dried garlic powder is less likely to burn off and get bitter, as fresh garlic does, and it is a convenient way to add a punch of savoriness to marinades and rubs.

ONION POWDER: Onion powder is three times more potent than dried onion, so remember to use this stuff carefully.

OREGANO: Oregano is Mexico's favorite dried herb to use when making stews, salsas, and marinades. It's worth seeking out Mexican oregano for its slightly citrusy and pungent flavor that's deeper than its more subtle Italian oregano variant, which tends to taste sweeter.

Vegetables

NOPALES: There is no greater vegetable to grill in a carne asada than whole nopal paddles, which are the thin stalks of the same cactus that gives us tuna fruit (also called prickly pears). When cooked over a roaring fire, nopalitos take on a meaty texture, and the high heat cooks out most of the slime and increases their unique sour flavor. Plus, they are virtually impossible to overcook because they have so much moisture. Look for nopales that are thin and dark green. If in a time crunch, opt for buying pre-packaged nopal paddles that are sold already shaved of their prickly thorns.

RADISH: A radish never tastes as good as when eaten in between mouthfuls of your carne asada. Its refreshing and spicy bite is the best contrast you can ask for and it tastes great simply sliced, dressed with fresh lime juice, and sprinkled with salt. You can always count on sliced radishes with a little lime and salt as a side dish to serve with any kind of grilled meat featured in this cookbook. Look for radishes that have bright-green tops with no signs of wilting.

SPRING ONIONS, GREEN ONIONS, AND SCALLIONS: A carne asada is not complete without the smoky and sweet subtle flavor of any variety of a charred green onion. Always buy more than what you think you will need, because they are so delicious they are often the first item to run out. A small bunch is usually enough for two people. They do well under low and slow cooking on the edges of the grill, so don't take up any vital space during peak heat that can be used for meat. Look for green onions that do not have any brown edges or sagging green stalks.

TOMATILLOS: Tomatillos are essential to a carne asada for their high acid and refreshing flavor when transformed into a salsa. Prepping a tomatillo is pretty straightforward. The husks can be easily removed with your hands and discarded. The sticky film on the surface of the fruit comes off with a quick rinse under water. For all recipes, we recommend the marble-size milpero variety of tomatillos over the standard tomatillos, which are twice their size, for their slightly sweeter flavor and lesser water content, but the bigger ones are fine if milperos are not available. For milperos, look for tomatillos that aren't wrinkled and that have a dark-purple leopard pattern. For big ones, look for tomatillos that don't have any blemishes underneath the husk. They can be blended raw for an exceptionally tart salsa, boiled for a sweeter salsa, and fire-grilled or roasted for a smokier salsa.

Tortillas: Corn or Flour?

The answer to this perpetual question is the equivalent of trying to figure out the meaning of life. The reality is that it will forever be a case-by-case basis depending on your mood and what part of Mexico your family is from. For the longest time, there was a preconceived notion that flour tortillas were less authentic than corn. I was one of the people who believed this. But my husband grew up in Calexico, and all he ever knew were flour tortillas. If eating asada in Sonora, it is practically impossible to find tacos de asada on corn tortillas. If eating *tasajo asado* (thinly sliced beef) in Oaxaca, your carne asada will be served with a pile of tlayuda-size *blandas* made from nixtamal (see page 51 for my Homemade Tlayuditas), and it is impossible find a flour version there. In states like Baja California and Sinaloa, you can find both.

I'm happy that our children will grow up with the privilege of enjoying both flour and corn tortillas.

The quality of both corn and flour tortillas has been going down steadily in the United States since the first packaged tortilla was sold on a supermarket shelf in the early 1970s. That was when tortillas got the American convenience treatment. Instead of tortillas made the traditional way, with just nixtamalized corn or flour, water, and, for flour tortillas, a small amount of salt and fat, manufacturers started pumping them full of additives and preservatives. This newer formula was built to last months on a supermarket shelf, but the additives and preservatives took away a tortilla's soul. In Mexico, it's still easy to find corn tortillas made with local maize varieties. Each type of corn offers unique colors, smells, and flavors when made

into tortillas. If not making tortillas by hand, when shopping for tortillas, look for labels that have the fewest ingredients. For corn tortillas, all you need is corn, water, and lime. For flour tortillas, all you need is wheat, water, salt, and fat. Anything else added beyond these ingredients will ultimately affect the flavor and texture of a tortilla.

When hosting your backyard carne asada, your guests will love either option you end up choosing. If you want to be the carne asada host with the most, you can offer both corn and flour tortillas and let your guests mix it up.

A Guide to Mexican Dairy

Dairy products play a crucial supporting role when hosting a carne asada. They provide a welcoming contrast to all the meat in your taco, and for vegetarians, the dairy options can be their whole world. Mexico quickly made cheese into a staple food after it was introduced by Spain in the 1500s. There have been so many regional styles and textures found all over Mexico. A handful of these cheeses made the migration to the United States, many times in the suitcases of immigrants from Mexico who brought their hometown favorites into cities like Los Angeles, Chicago, and New York.

As immigrants started families and went back to Mexico less and less, some went on to start their own Mexican cheese to keep the culture alive for the next generation. To this day, cheese is still a love language among many Mexican families, and yes it is still common to bring back cheese in your suitcase from Mexico because it just hits different. And remember, buying pre-shredded anything is never worth it. Here is a guide on essential Mexican dairy to have in your kitchen and in your carne asada.

QUESO FRESCO: Queso fresco is the most popular and versatile Mexican cheese. It first made an appearance in American supermarkets in the early 1970s. Its snow-white curds pressed into a small wheel stood out among all the cheddars and processed cheese singles in the cheese section. It is also the easiest Mexican cheese to find across supermarkets around the country. It is often defined as a fresh farmer's cheese, but Mexican style: slightly milky, bouncy, and with a neutral flavor that helps tie everything together. It doesn't really melt, but it does intensify in flavor when heated. It can be cubed and slipped into a poblano chile, roasted, and served as an appetizer or another element in your carne asada plate. It can also be crumbled on top of beans, on top of your tostada, or used as a layer in your torta. It's a good idea to always have queso fresco on deck. Sometimes a warm tortilla with a slice of queso fresco and a dollop of salsa is all you need to keep going.

COTIJA: Often referred to as "Mexican parmesan," cotija is a potent-smelling aged cheese best when crumbled and used to finish a dish. Its roots go back to Cotija de La Paz, Michoacán, where it is cubed and typically served to snack on wherever you order mezcal. In the United States, a wedge of the stuff goes a long way. It adds an instant boost of salty umami flavor to anything it touches.

QUESO OAXACA: The main difference between queso Oaxaca and quesillo is that the former is pasteurized and not made in its town of origin, Oaxaca. This is due to stringent American laws that do not allow the sale of semi-fresh unpasteurized cheeses for sale. The latter is a Mexican-inspired cheese that is more like American-style string cheese. It melts beautifully and creates picturesque cheese pulls. This is the cheese you want when making chiles rellenos, queso fundido, or quesadillas.

QUESO ENCHILADO: This is a unique aged cheese. It is not as widely available as other Mexican-style cheeses, but it is so good that it is worth ordering online to taste. It is essentially a slightly less salty cotija that has been dipped in paprika or chile powder to develop an alluring red hue and peppery flavor throughout the cheese. It is descended from Spain's traditional hard cheeses that were dipped in smoked pimentón powder to aid the curing process. In rural Mexican communities, pimentón was switched out with a chile paste made from dried red chiles. We recommend using this chile anywhere you would use cotija. However, because it is less salty, it is also delicious enough just sliced on a toasted tortilla.

REQUESÓN: This is a lesser-known Mexican cheese that is soft enough to be spreadable but also firm enough to stand on its own on a cheese plate. The closest equivalent is ricotta cheese, but requesón has less moisture. In large cities, this cheese is the newest to be widely available. In Mexico, it has a connotation of being a lighter choice of cheese because it doesn't have as much fat as other cheeses. In states like Jalisco, requesón is typically a filling in tacos dorados. In Oaxaca, it is eaten with fruits. It can be a base for cheesecakes as well, and it tastes great spread on toast with jam the next morning, too.

CREMA MEXICANA: Mexican-style sour cream is thinner in texture than American sour cream. It is also richer in flavor, with a natural sweetness due to its culturing process. With its buttery flavor, it steps into the realm of a crème fraîche, but because it is not as thick, it can be drizzled over food to add a cooling creaminess that hits the spot when eating lots of chiles. It is also versatile and can be used in both savory and sweet dishes, like in bionicos (a dessert parfait with fresh cream, page 255) or fresas (strawberries) con crema.

CREMA SALVADOREÑA: This Salvadorian-style crema is thicker, creamier, and saltier than Mexican-style crema. It is also tangier and thick enough to be spooned on top of food. It is a great variation to mix up your crema game at home and is my crema of choice when I'm making savory dishes.

A Guide to all the Chicharrón

Aside from *totopos* (tortilla chips), chicharrón is the best botana to welcome your guests to your carne asada. Since it is essentially pig skin slowly fried in oil or lard until crispy, all chicharrón is delicious, but there are actually many chicharrón styles to choose from. Here is a simple breakdown to help you choose the best one for each of your needs.

CHICHARRÓN DE TIRITAS, aka chicharrón botanero: This is the most common kind of chicharrón in Mexico and the U.S. This style is cut into thick strips and is similar to American-style pork rinds because it can be snacked on as is. In Mexican supermarkets, these are sometimes sold by the pound in plastic bags on top of the butcher case.

CHICHARRÓN DELGADO: This chicharrón has the most puffy texture and makes the most stunning presentation because the chicharrón is left whole in sheets. It really lends itself to a communal snacking experience because you have to tear it with your hands and share all the jagged pieces. It is also the best type of chicharrón to serve with salsas because you can really load it up.

CHICHARRÓN CARNUDO: This chicharrón stands out from the rest because it is the only kind that still has meat attached to the skin. This adds a nice jerky-like meatiness to your usual crispy bite of chicharrón. It is a spectacular style that is substantial enough to be a taco, eaten as-is on top of a warm tortilla. It is also a great chicharrón to stew in salsa.

CHICHARRÓN MORUZA: This chicharrón is the leanest of them all since it is practically all meat that is given the chicharrón treatment. This one is best cubed.

CHICHARRÓN PRENSADO: This unique chicharrón style is common in Mexico City and surrounding central states. It is essentially chicharrón carnudo that is pressed tightly right after frying, which squeezes out all the excess lard it was fried in. The result is a chicharrón that resembles more European-style rillette. It is usually stewed in a salsa and it is the meatiest of the chicharrón kingdom.

The Asada Cuts

Carne asada is beautifully unpretentious. It's the opposite of going to a fancy steakhouse where you're presented with a menu offering all of the expensive cuts you can imagine. Most of the cuts for your typical carne asada meats can be found at your local supermarket. Most of the recipes in this book were tested with USDA Prime-grade beef, pasture-raised whenever possible. Remember that fat is flavor! Always look for marbling in your beef. If this quality of beef is not readily available, recipes that rely on a heavy marinade come in handy. When done properly, marinades have the ability to break down protein and tenderize any meat.

Here is a guide to all the meats in our recipes.

FLAP STEAK: Also known as *ranchera*, this is the most popular cut of beef you will see in any backyard carne asada. It would even be fair to call this the king cut of carne asada because it is so versatile and affordable. When it's on the thicker side, you can season and grill it until medium-rare, and when it's on the thinner side, you can leave it on the grill a little longer so it chars up until the edges are crispy and delicious. Some people love thick-cut asada and others prefer thinner and more jerky-like. Both are great options. Look for flap steaks that are deeply and brightly red.

SKIRT STEAK: Also known as *arrachera* in Español, this cut is very similar to flap steak, but it is thicker and can also be eaten like a steak. It has a more intense beefy flavor. It's vital to cut the meat very thinly across the grain, and it is at its best when it's not cooked much past medium-rare. Look for skirt steaks that have even marbling and are at least ½ inch (12 mm) thick.

RIB EYE: Rib eye almost needs no introduction. It is a prized cut of beef renowned for its perfect meat-to-fat ratio and a thickness that's just right to throw on a grill. You'll see this cut used for carne asada in Mexico's northern capital cities like Hermosillo and Monterrey, or at special *asaderos* (taco steakhouses) where you can choose whether you want arrachera or a rib-eye cut for your carne asada taco. When grilling it at home, its high price demands for it to be reserved for special occasions. Look for Prime-grade thick steaks because if you're going big, you might as well go all out. We recommend seasoning these beautiful steaks with just salt and pepper to let its pristine beefiness shine.

FLANKEN BEEF COSTILLITAS: This beef cut is the MVP of carne asada cuts for a number of reasons. It is the most forgiving cut, which will almost always yield tender and beefy goodness, no matter how many times you flip it or forget to flip it. And it is almost universally liked, whether it's seasoned simply or marinated. Not to mention that it is also really affordable and provides the gratification that can only be achieved when you eat bone-in meat.

MEXICAN CHORIZO: A carne asada is not complete without a couple of chorizo links to throw on the grill and char up. Mexican chorizo is uncured and raw, and usually made out of ground pork, but there are beef and chicken versions available. Highly seasoned with dried chiles and spices, the flavor is also bright, thanks to ample use of vinegar in the ground meat. You'll find chorizo available for sale by the pound in Mexican markets or packaged in the refrigerated section, usually next to deli meats. Look for chorizo that is enclosed in a pork casing, since the chorizo that is sold without a casing can be cooked in a pan but not on a grill. Note: Soy-based vegetarian chorizo is sold in a plastic casing, which cannot be grilled. This plant-based alternative needs to be sauteed in a nonstick pan with a little bit of oil, but can crisp up into a very meat-like texture. You can also substitute Salvadoran-style chorizo or longaniza, which are other delicious forms of cased chorizo that use a different blend of dried chiles and spices.

SPANISH CHORIZO: Spanish chorizo is probably the variety that most people are used to eating. It is made out of pork and seasoned mostly with *pimentón* (paprika). It is cured and ready to slice and eat, though you can also fry it a bit to render its savory paprika flavor into other foods like our Frijoles Charros (page 132), potatoes, or any stew.

LAMB SHOULDER: Mexicans love eating lamb. Lamb shoulder is a lean cut meant for long-term cooking and benefits greatly from being slowly braised or stewed under low heat. In Mexico, you'll usually find it braised or roasted in barbacoa form. In the United States, lamb is not as popular as beef, but it is incredibly satisfying when you are craving red meat and want something a little different. It is usually imported from New Zealand or Australia and tends to be pasture-fed, which explains why the flavor can be strong-tasting to some. When buying lamb, look for meat that is dark pink with layers of creamy white fat.

PORK CHOP: In asada culture, it's easy to get super obsessed with beef and chicken and forget that pork also benefits from being grilled with smoke and fire. Pork chops aren't traditional in carne asadas but we love throwing a few thick-cut chops on the grill. Pork chops are naturally lean, so it is all about practice and trusting your meat thermometer when it comes to figuring out how long to grill them to reach your ideal vision of doneness. When it comes to buying pork, try to go organic for the best and cleanest flavor.

PORK LOIN: This is a straightforward cut of pork that is lean and easy to grill. It benefits from being tenderized via pounding and marinating.

SKINLESS CHICKEN BREAST: Good ole chicken breast is always there for you whenever you need some quick and easy protein. We usually opt for organic or free-range since we have found that they have a deeper chicken flavor. When shopping for chicken, look for meat that is nice and pink, as chicken tends to get grayer the older it gets.

BONE-IN CHICKEN THIGHS WITH SKIN: This is arguably the best chicken cut because it is so affordable and delicious. The "dark meat" muscle is considered a tougher cut, although it also has a higher amount of fat—way more than lean chicken breast. This translates into a rich flavor and tender texture that is almost impossible to overcook. The skin acts as a protective shield of sorts to prevent the chicken from drying out.

Choosing Your Grilling Style and the Reason Why Your Tío Cleans the Grill with an Onion

Mastering the art of a carne asada and getting to know your grill takes time, practice, and dedication. Overcooking a few pieces of meat, charring a few vegetables, or burning your hand is all part of the process. But before you decide on a grill, you need to learn the art of using an onion to clean the grill grate.

Cleaning your grill is one of the most important parts of a carne asada ritual. It's easy to dismiss using an onion to clean the grill as something your drunk tío used to do because he was too lazy to actually clean the grill, but you would be surprised to find out that he was onto something: Onions contain a surprisingly high amount of an antimicrobial compound named allicin.

The cooking grid is much easier to clean when it is still warm. So get your grill super hot first to burn off any remaining charred asada bits and pieces and make it easier to scrub. Then, using a grilling fork stuck with half a yellow onion, scrub up and down the grilling grid until all the gunk has been removed. For extra gunk-fighting power, you can spray the grates with lemon juice or white vinegar first. The extra acidity helps the cleaning process. Never doubt Mexican wisdom ever again. Note: If you plan to grill a sweet dish or dessert next, maybe it is best to use a stainless steel scrubber.

Carbón (Charcoal)

From portable camping grills to your reliable Weber grill that has been passed down to you and all the fancy new-school grills that offer you optimum smoke and temperature regulation, charcoal grills are the most common in backyard carne asadas. They are available in all shapes and sizes, are easy to use and clean, and provide meat with that smoky flavor that everyone associates with a carne asada. Our favorite type of charcoal is lump mesquite, because not only is it the most traditional, we've found that it imparts the most flavor. If you're all about the ritual behind carne asada, this type of grill is for you. Here are some tips to help you optimize your carne asada cooking experience using a charcoal grill.

• Always make sure to clean out the ashes after the burnt charcoal has cooled down.

• Buy a cover for it to protect it from rain and other elements.

• To light your charcoal, we recommend buying and familiarizing yourself with a chimney starter. We do not recommend using lighter fluid, as convenient as it may be to get your fire started, because of the chemicals that do not break down easily and the potential for them to get absorbed by your meat as it grills. It usually takes about 15 to 20 minutes to get the charcoal preheated and ready for grilling.

• When emptying your chimney starter full of hot charcoal (using a grilling glove, ideally), try to carefully empty it out in the middle of your grill in a pyramid shape. You can use your grilling tongs to carefully move the coals around before they get too hot. This willl create two cooking zones: one for direct and high-heat cooking (directly over the coals), and another for medium- to lower-heat cooking (off to the sides). You can continue cooking it on the edge of your grill until your preferred doneness is reached without burning your meat. Or use the lower-heat areas to slowly grill vegetables to bring out all of their natural sugars without scorching them.

• To have a reserve of hot coals ready to go, to replenish your direct cooking space in case the coals start to die, using a grilling glove, carefully lift up the cooking grid and pour some unheated coals around the edges of your grill. As the charcoal turns white, it will be ready to add to your main grilling area if you need more heat.

• As a rule of thumb, 5 pounds (2.3 kg) of mesquite lump charcoal will provide about 2 hours of cooking time—enough time to grill some meats and vegetables for four to six people.

Gas

Gas grills are not my favorite, but they are undoubtedly the most convenient option for a carne asada, especially if you live in a condo or apartment where you may have only a small outdoor space available for grilling. While you won't achieve that smoky flavor you get from a charcoal grill, the upside is that you will most likely have carne asada much more often due to the home stove–like convenience of a gas grill. If you're an everyday carne asada type of person and find yourself making a mess all over your stove because you grill meat often, this type of grill is best for you. Here are some tips to help you optimize your carne asada cooking experience using a gas grill.

• This one sounds like a no-brainer, but always make sure to fill your propane tank with enough gas for your grilling session.

• After about six months of consistent grilling (two to three carne asadas a month), you may start to get a fat deposit inside the grill, which will cause flare-ups and uneven cooking. To prevent this, make sure to do a deep-clean of your grill at least twice a year.

• Preheat your gas grill for at least 15 minutes before using it to make sure it is at its hottest to cook your carne asada evenly.

Electric and Pellet Grills

The newest and nicest types of grills available in the carne asada game, electric and pellet smokers offer convenience and, in the case of pellet smokers, smoky flavor, too. Think of these fancy grills as outdoor convection ovens that you can just plug into an electric outlet and go. In some high-end brands like Traeger, you can sync your phone's Bluetooth to your grill so you can control the temperature from anywhere in your home. If you're all about having the latest and greatest equipment and love to grill with very minimal effort, this type of grill is for you. Here are some tips to help you optimize your carne asada cooking experience using a pellet grill.

• When using a new pellet smoker for the first time, remember to run it for at least 30 to 45 minutes to "season" it by burning off any residues from the manufacturing process.

• Lower temperatures generate more smoke flavor. But a pellet grill can easily reach searingly hot temperatures quickly as well. Take advantage of the ease of temperature flexibility by trying different grilling methods like reverse searing, which is when you slowly cook a piece of meat under low temperatures and then sear it to finish.

• Experiment with using pellets made from different kinds of wood to find which smoke flavors you prefer paired with certain meats and vegetables.

Starters

Think of botanas as pregaming for carne asada. Your grill doesn't need to be on for most of the recipes, and they are perfect for your guests who are on time while you are still working on the finishing touches.

LAS BOTANAS

Frutero Salad

Serves 8

Driving or walking around Los Angeles, you will notice fruit vendors who set up shop in corners around every neighborhood of the city. They are entrepreneurs who are always there to provide cold, sliced fresh fruit that is dependably ripe on a hot day. Some people call them Mexican fruit vendors, but I genuinely dislike the description. I do love how they dress their ripe fruit: lime juice, salt, and chile powder. I go to one who posts up on the corner of Figureoa and Avenue 57 in Highland Park. The recipe is a street-style fruit salad and an easy spread to have ready for guests. I like to serve the fruit in recyclable cups, so each guest can claim their own. Also, don't discard the juices at the bottom of the cup—instead pour them over your michelada mix (page 71) and thank me later.

1 medium **jicama** (25 ounces/750 g), quartered and peeled

1 small **seedless watermelon** (6 pounds/2.7 kg), quartered and peeled

1 small **pineapple** (3 pounds/1.4 kg), peeled, quartered, and cored

2 semi-ripe **mangoes** (5¼ ounces each/150 g), peeled, halved, and pitted

7 **Persian cucumbers**, peels on

Juice of 2 **key limes**

Flaky sea salt

Chile-lime salt

¼ cup (60 ml) **chamoy sauce** (preferably homemade; recipe on page 213)

Bottles of chile lime seasoning are usually found near the fruit section at your local Mexican supermarket. The most popular brand name is Tajín.

Cut the jicama, watermelon, pineapple, mangoes, into uniform spears, about 1 inch (2.5 cm) thick by 4 inches (10 cm) long. Slice the cucumber into ½-inch thick rounds. Toss the fruit in a large bowl with the key lime juice. Distribute an even amount of fruit in eight 6-ounce (180 ml) cups, so guests can sip the juice after the fruit is gone. Finish each with a generous sprinkle of sea salt flakes, chile-lime salt, and chamoy.

Cheese and Chicharrón Board

Serves 12

A charcuterie board at a carne asada is out of place, but a board piled high with crunchy chicharrón and all your favorite quesos sets the stage for the rest of the party. This recipe is inspired by my father's go-to snack whenever he has *visitas* (company): roughly chopped quesillo cubes on a plate topped with a can of jalapeños with plenty of its brine, too. If you were ever to visit him, he would probably also go to the corner store to buy some freshly fried irresistible chicharrón and lay it out along with this cheese and some warm tortillas. This is our kind of meat-and-cheese board.

1 cup (240 ml) **Salsa Taquera en Molcajete** (page 193)

1 cup (240 ml) **Salsa Verde** (page 184)

4 cups (640 g) **Cauliflower and Jalapeño en Escabeche** (page 38)

2 cups (480 ml) **Guacamole Tatemado en Molcajete** (page 43)

Tortillas (preferably homemade; recipes on pages 46–51)

10 ounces (285 g) **queso fresco**, sliced

10 ounces (285 g) **queso Oaxaca**

8 ounces (225 g) **queso requesón**, loosely separated with your fingertips

10 ounces (285 g) **queso enchilado**, cut into wedges

7 ounces (200 g) **chicharrón botanero**

7 ounces (200 g) **chicharrón delgado**

8 ounces (250 g) **chicharrón carnudo** (with meat attached)

8 ounces (250 g) **chicharrón moruza** (with fat)

Place the salsas, escabeche, and guacamole in serving bowls. Heat up your tortillas in a skillet and transfer them to a tortilla warmer or wrap in a kitchen cloth. Lay out all of the cheeses and chicharrón on a board, spacing them evenly. Place the tortillas next to the board and serve. Best enjoyed within 3 to 4 hours.

Cauliflower and Jalapeño en Escabeche

Makes 4 cups (640 g)

Carne asada is for meat lovers, but some vegetables are crucial to a proper carne asada, like grilled spring onions and nopales. If you love canned jalapeños, this homemade version of pickled jalapeños with cauliflower and more is a game changer because it's a lot easier to prepare than you think. I serve this with our Cheese and Chicharrón Board (page 36) because it cuts the richness and keeps you coming back for more. The best part is that you will usually have leftovers, and you can snack on them later when you realize you ate way too much meat—again.

¼ cup (60 ml) **olive oil**

6 **jalapeños** (3½ ounces/100 g), halved lengthwise, seeded, and sliced into strips

4 **carrots** (8¾ ounces/250 g), peeled and sliced 1 inch (2.5 cm) thick

4 small **cloves garlic**, peeled and smashed

2 sprigs **thyme**

1 **bay leaf**

¼ teaspoon **dried marjoram**

4 teaspoons **sea salt**

½ cup (120 ml) **pineapple vinegar** (can substitute a citrus vinegar)

½ cup (120 ml) **apple cider vinegar**

1½ teaspoons **demerara cane sugar**

1 small head **cauliflower** (14 ounces/400 g), cut into small florets

1 small **habanero chile**, thinly sliced

½ small **jicama** (9¼ ounces/260 g), peeled and sliced 1 inch (2.5 cm) thick

Citrus vinegar is more subtle than apple cider vinegar. You can find them online or at well-stocked supermarkets like Whole Foods.

Heat the oil in a wide pot over medium heat. Once hot, add the jalapeños and carrots. Sauté for 3 minutes, until the jalapeños release their aroma. Add the garlic, thyme, bay leaf, marjoram, and salt. Sauté for another 5 minutes. Add the pineapple and cider vinegars, the sugar, and ¼ cup (60 ml) water and keep sautéing until the ingredients are well combined. Stir in the cauliflower, habanero, and jicama and sauté for 5 minutes.

Turn off the heat.

Transfer to a bowl, cover, and let rest for at least 3 hours, stirring once every hour. Refrigerate until ready to serve. This will keep for up to 4 weeks in the refrigerator.

Blended Guacamole

Makes 2 cups (480 ml)

Guacamole is carne asada's best friend. This variation is inspired by the version served in my family's restaurant and my mother's love for oregano. We don't use tomato because it can make it too watery. The base of this guacamole is blended first, then the avocado is added afterward. This creates a more uniform and versatile texture that can be universally enjoyed in a taco, with our Cheese and Chicharrón Board (page 36), with grilled seafood, or anything really. We never shy away from chile or lime juice. If your blender has trouble blending everything, you can add a bit of water to help it get started.

6 tablespoons (90 ml) **fresh lime juice**
1 teaspoon **sea salt**
1 cup (40 g) **fresh cilantro**
1 **serrano chile**, stem removed
¼ teaspoon **dried oregano**
3 **avocados**, pitted and peeled

Put the lime juice, salt, cilantro, chile, and oregano in a blender and blend until smooth.

In a large mixing bowl, mash the avocados and pour the lime juice over the top.

Mix until everything is well combined. Serve with *totopos* (tortilla chips).

Guacamole Tatemado en Molcajete

Makes 2 cups (480 ml)

How do you perfect something that is already perfect? Charred spring onions are the MVP at a carne asada. They require patience, but their tender, sweet, and smoky flavor is the perfect bite to follow up juicy carne asada. We take these onions and roughly crush them with lime and salt to add another layer of texture and flavor to guacamole. The result is an extra-buttery guacamole without the sharp bite of the usual raw onion. If you don't own a molcajete, you can use the bottom of a cup and a mixing bowl instead.

10 **green onions** or **spring onions** (6 ounces/165 g)
Sea salt
1 **serrano chile**, finely chopped, or more to taste
2 tablespoons finely chopped **fresh cilantro**
1 tablespoon finely chopped **fresh mint**
2 ripe **avocados**, halved, pitted, and flesh
   scooped out
1 tablespoon **fresh lime juice**

Preheat your grill to 425°F (220°C) if using a pellet grill, to high heat if using gas, or for direct cooking if using charcoal, with the lid closed, for 15 minutes.

Add the onions to the grill and cook, flipping them once in a while, for about 15 minutes, or until they have charred evenly. Remove the onions from the grilling grid and season them generously with salt.

Place the charred onions, chile, cilantro, and mint in a molcajete and roughly mash with a pestle until the onions have broken down. Add the avocado and continue mashing until you reach a chunky consistency. Finish with the lime and season to taste with salt.

Papas Caseras en Bolsa

Serves 6

Freshly fried potato chips are a simple and thoughtful welcome snack at a party. Their addictive crispness often sparks conversations about everyone's own memories around eating papitas. Making them at home is a dying art because of the convenience of all the delicious packaged potato chips at the grocery store, but homemade chips just hit differently. Some chips have brown edges and other chips puff up; it's all part of the thrill. The bona fide Mexican way of eating papas is by squeezing on lots of fresh lime juice and a traditional vinegar-based bottled Mexican hot sauce. Then proceed to devour them uncontrollably because they are so irresistible.

---

4 **russet potatoes** (3½ pounds/1.6 kg), peeled
¼ cup (60 ml) **distilled white vinegar**
2 quarts (2 L) **peanut oil**
Sea salt
1 **lime**

For the garnish:
Bottled hot sauce

Using a mandoline with the thinnest blade available, slice the potatoes. Place them in a large bowl and cover with the vinegar and about 6 cups (1.4 L) water. Allow to rest for 30 to 45 minutes in the vinegar water. Drain and pat dry.

Fit a medium-size heavy pot with a thermometer and pour in the oil. Preheat over medium-high until the thermometer registers 300°F (150°C).

Working in batches, and returning the oil to 300°F (150°C) between batches, fry the potatoes, stirring with a spider or slotted spoon occasionally to ensure they cook evenly, until golden brown and crisp, about 5 minutes per batch. Using the same spoon, transfer to a paper towel–lined plate. Season with salt.

Divide the chips evenly into individual portions and finish with a squeeze of lime and a drizzle of the hot sauce.

Avocado Oil Flour Tortillas

Makes 8 Tortillas

Flour tortillas are an art, and the more you make them, the better your tortilla will get. There is something extremely satisfying about making your own from scratch, unlike many of the packaged flour tortillas out there. This one—inspired by Caramelo tortillería in Lawrence, Kansas—only takes three ingredients. Using avocado oil is a more recent substitute to old-school ingredients like lard or vegetable shortening.

2 cups (260 g) **all-purpose flour**, plus more for dusting

1 teaspoon **sea salt**

¼ cup (60 ml) **avocado oil**

In a large bowl, stir together the flour and salt with a fork to combine. Pour in the oil and ¾ cup (180 ml) water and stir with a rubber spatula to incorporate. Allow the dough to rest for 5 minutes and then knead it until smooth. Divide the dough into 8 pieces and roll each piece into a ball. Place the balls in a well-floured bowl and cover them with a kitchen towel to rest for about 30 minutes before shaping the tortillas.

On a well-floured surface, roll each ball of dough into a 10-inch (25 cm) disc using a rolling pin.

Preheat a large cast-iron pan over medium-high heat. When the pan is hot, place a tortilla on the pan and cook it for 30 to 45 seconds, or until small bubbles start to form. Flip it over with your hands or a spatula and cook for another 30 to 45 seconds. Remove from the pan and place it in a tortilla warmer or wrap in a kitchen towel. Repeat with the remaining dough. Serve immediately.

Corn Tortillas

Makes 12 Tortillas

Homemade corn tortillas are easier than most people imagine them to be. I always make the comparison that people take the time to make pancakes, yet they've never tried flipping a handmade tortilla. Look for high-quality tortilla flour. At Guelaguetza, my family's online store, we sell the perfect tortilla flour made from heirloom Oaxacan corn.

2 cups (230 g) **masa harina flour**
1 teaspoon **sea salt**
1½ cups (360 ml) **warm water**

In a large bowl, stir together the flour and salt with a fork to combine. Pour in the water and knead with your hands until you achieve a dough-like texture. The masa should feel moist but not sticky or runny. Form 12 even balls of masa—about 2 inches (5 cm) in diameter each—and set aside.

Press each ball individually on a plastic wrap–lined tortilla press. Each tortilla should be about 6 inches (15 cm) in diameter after pressing.

On the stovetop, bring a comal or cast-iron skillet to medium heat. When hot, carefully place each tortilla, one at a time, on the comal or skillet and cook each side for about 2 minutes, until the edges start to brown a bit. Using your fingertips, apply a little bit of pressure to the tortilla as each side is cooking. Flip the tortilla a couple more times until the center starts to lightly brown as well, and transfer to a tortilla warmer or wrap in kitchen cloth to keep them warm. Note: A tortilla does not always puff up during cooking. This is OK.

49

Tostadas fried in duck fat and peanut oil

Handmade flour tortillas

Tlayuditas

Handmade corn tortillas

Homemade Tlayuditas

Makes 10

There is always a special place in your heart for tlayudas if you have any roots in Oaxaca. I went back and forth a lot on whether I should name this a mini tlayuda or a tostada, since it is not a proper tlayuda unless it is made in Oaxaca! However, I'm aware that many of us won't have the luxury of enjoying a fresh-made tlayuda every day. This is my adaptation of Oaxaca's sacred oversized tortilla using high-quality masa harina (tortilla flour) and the tlayuda-making techniques I learned growing up.

2 cups (230 g) **masa harina flour**
1 teaspoon **sea salt**
1 cup plus 6 tablespoons (330 ml) **warm water**

In a large bowl, stir together the flour and salt with a fork to combine. Add the water and knead with your hands until you achieve a dough-like texture. The masa should feel moist but not sticky or runny. Form 12 even balls of masa—about 1 ounce (25 g), 2 inches (5 cm) each—and set aside.

Preheat the oven to 350°F (175°C).

Press each ball of dough individually on a plastic wrap–lined tortilla press. Each tortilla should be about 6 inches (15 cm) in diameter after pressing.

On the stovetop, bring a comal or cast-iron skillet to medium heat. When hot, carefully place each tortilla, one at a time, on the comal or skillet, cooking for about 2 minutes on each side, to partially cook each tortilla. Flip the tortilla a couple more times until the center starts to lightly brown as well and transfer to a cooling rack.

Place the tortillas, evenly spaced, directly onto the middle rack of the preheated oven. (It's important to not use a baking sheet; this will allow the tlayudas to dry out as they toast in the oven). Bake for 8 to 10 minutes, or until the tortillas start to turn a light brown, flipping halfway through.

Remove from the oven and allow the tlayudas to cool on a cooling rack.

Tostadas Caseras (Homemade Tostadas)

Makes 12

A tostada is one of those things that we take for granted. There are so many great packaged ones out there, but that moment when you bite into a super flaky homemade tostada will immediately make you think: *Why didn't I fry my own tortillas before?* The texture is so delicate, and it instantly makes all the things you pile it high with all the better. We use duck fat in ours to add an extra layer of savory richness.

½ cup (120 ml) **rendered duck fat**
½ cup (120 ml) **peanut oil**
12 **corn tortillas** (preferably homemade; recipes on pages 48 and 51)
2 teaspoons **sea salt**

In a medium frying pan over medium heat, add the duck fat and oil. When the fat is hot, working in batches, gently add the corn tortillas. Let them cook until they're golden brown then flip them, using tongs to push the tortilla down, about 1 minute per side.

Lower the heat to low. Remove the tortillas and place them on a wide plate or cooling rack lined with paper towels; sprinkle the salt on top while the tortillas are still warm. You can strain the duck fat and oil mixture through a fine-mesh sieve and reserve it in a mason jar for another use.

Cucumber and Queso Fresco Salad

Serves 6

The first time my mom told me about this salad, I have to be honest, the ingredient list did not look appealing. Then one day I hosted an asada after work on a hot summer afternoon to welcome some friends who were visiting from Oaxaca. I was looking for something quick and refreshing to have on the table. It's tricky when it comes to appetizers, because you want to serve something guests will love but not something so heavy that it will take away from the main dish. This salad is perfect for that. The combination just works.

¼ cup (105 g) **Pickled Red Onions** (page 159; can substitute raw onions soaked in water)

1 **serrano chile**, finely chopped

¾ cup (30 g) finely chopped **fresh cilantro**

1½ pounds (680 g) **Persian cucumbers**, cut into 1-inch (2.5 cm) slices

10 ounces (285 g) **queso fresco**, crumbled

Juice of 3 **key limes** (about 2 tablespoons)

½ teaspoon **sea salt**

In a large bowl, toss the pickled onions with the chile and the cilantro. Add the cucumbers and queso fresco. Toss and season with the key lime juice and sea salt. Let rest in the refrigerator and serve cold.

Grilled Salpicón Tostadas

Serves 6

This is a grilled version of the traditional Mexican-style pulled beef salad. It can be made a day ahead. This dish is also ideal to make for a weeknight dinner. The leftovers make an incredible lunch the next day.

---

2 teaspoons **sea salt**

1 teaspoon **ground cumin**

½ teaspoon **freshly ground black pepper**

½ teaspoon **garlic powder**

½ teaspoon **onion powder**

2 pounds (910 g) **beef flank steak**, cut into 2 equal pieces

2 **serrano chiles**, finely chopped

2 **Fresno chiles**, finely chopped

½ cup (60 g) thinly sliced **red onion**

½ cup (20 g) finely chopped **fresh cilantro leaves**

¼ cup (13 g) finely chopped **fresh mint leaves**

1 tablespoon **dried oregano**

1 cup (30 g) shredded **butter lettuce**

1 cup (130 g) thinly sliced **radishes**

2 tablespoons **citrus vinegar**

¼ cup (60 ml) **fresh lime juice**

½ cup (120 ml) **olive oil**

Tostadas (preferably homemade; recipe on page 52)

For the garnishes:
Crumbled **queso fresco**
1 **avocado**, pitted, cubed, and peeled

Mix the salt, cumin, pepper, garlic powder, and onion powder in a small bowl. Pat the steak dry with paper towels, then sprinkle the rub evenly over both sides, gently patting to help it stick. Let sit for at least 15 minutes.

Preheat your grill to 375°F (190°C) if using a pellet grill, to low heat if using gas, or for indirect cooking if using charcoal, with the lid closed, for 15 minutes.

While the grill is heating, put the serrano and Fresno chiles, onion, cilantro, mint, oregano, lettuce, and radishes in a medium-size bowl and toss to combine. Toss well with the vinegar, lime juice, and olive oil to coat.

Put the steak on the grill directly over the fire. Close the lid and cook, turning once, about 4 to 5 minutes on each side. Transfer the meat to a cutting board and let rest for 5 minutes. Once the meat has cooled to the touch, finely shred it with your hands. Stir the shredded beef into the rest of the ingredients.

Scoop the beef mixture onto the tostadas and garnish with queso fresco and avocado.

Fingerling and Raja Tacos

Serves 12

Potatoes are probably the last thing you would have thought to throw on the grill, but imparting a bit of smoke to papas is a nice way to mix up this Mexican classic, beloved by everyone. Adding roasted poblano strips and shaved sweet corn contributes heat and sweetness. This taco is also substantial enough to be a main course for vegetarians at an asada. Going heavy on the crema and grated queso makes this taco all the better.

½ cup (120 ml) **extra-virgin olive oil**
1 teaspoon **onion powder**
1 teaspoon **garlic powder**
1 teaspoon plus 1 tablespoon **sea salt**, plus
    more as needed
½ teaspoon **dried parsley**
½ teaspoon **dried oregano**
½ teaspoon **ground mustard**
½ teaspoon **dried marjoram**
Juice of 1 **lemon** plus ½ its zest
1½ pounds (680 g) **fingerling potatoes**
1 large ear of **corn**
3 medium (10½ ounces/300 g) **poblano chiles**
Corn tortillas (preferably homemade: recipes
    on pages 48 and 51)
2 cups (480 ml) **peanut oil**

For the garnishes:
Grated **queso enchilado**
Mexican or **Salvadorian crema** (page 21)

Preheat your grill to 375°F (190°C) if using a pellet grill, to low heat if using gas, or for indirect cooking if using charcoal, with the lid closed, for 15 minutes.

In a large bowl, mix together the olive oil, onion powder, garlic powder, 1 teaspoon of salt, parsley, oregano, mustard, marjoram, and lemon juice and zest until thoroughly combined. Add the potatoes and mix well to coat.

Gently place the potatoes directly on the grill, alongside the ear of corn and poblanos. Reserve half the marinade in the bowl. Close the lid and allow the vegetables to cook until tender, about 20 minutes, making sure to flip them every once in a while to avoid burning.

Once the chiles and corn are evenly charred, after about 20 minutes, remove them from the grill. Put the chiles in a medium-size bowl and cover with a large plate for a few minutes to soften and steam them. This will make peeling off the burnt skin easier. When cool enough to handle, remove most of the skin from the chiles with your fingers. Remove and discard the seeds and stem and roughly chop the flesh. Remove the corn kernels by standing the cob upright and carefully shaving the kernels off from top to bottom using a chef's knife. Rotate the cob to make sure to shave all sides of the corn.

Once the potatoes are charred and tender, about 25 minutes, add them to a large bowl with the remaining 1 tablespoon salt, the roughly chopped poblanos, and the corn kernels. Smash everything with a potato masher until all the ingredients are smashed together in a chunky puree.

continued

Heat a large cast-iron skillet over medium heat. Working in batches, warm the tortillas for about 1 minute on each side so they soften. Remove them to a plate.

On a large cutting board, scoop about 2 table-spoons of the potato and poblano mixture onto each tortilla. Fold the tacos in half and set aside. Line a cooling rack with paper towels.

Heat the peanut oil in the cast-iron skillet over high heat. Test the oil for frying by dropping a small piece of tortilla in the middle; it should bubble up. Once the peanut oil is ready, using kitchen tongs, carefully (trying not to splash oil)drop in two or three tacos at a time, depending on the size of your skillet; be careful not to overcrowd the pan. Fry the tacos for about 3 minutes on each side, until crispy.

Remove each taco carefully using the kitchen tongs and place them on the cooling rack. Sprinkle with more salt. When cool enough to handle, top with the grated queso enchilado and crema and serve.

Meats

A great marinade or rub is magical. It has the power to make a cut of meat juicy and full of flavor. In the United States, we've become accustomed to buying marinated meats at the carnicería, but a carne asada is much more rewarding when you marinate the meat yourself.

LAS
CARNES

Carne Asada Clásica

Serves 4

It took me a couple attempts to get the umami level in this classic carne asada just right and hit that deep balance of savory flavors. I knew I finally got it right when my husband, who grew up eating this style of carne asada, couldn't stop eating it.

½ cup (120 ml) **orange juice**, freshly squeezed if in season
¼ cup (60 ml) **fresh lime juice**
¼ cup (60 ml) **grapeseed oil**
1 tablespoon **apple cider vinegar**
2½ teaspoons **Worcestershire sauce**
6 **cloves garlic**, minced
6 ounces (240 ml) **dark Mexican ale**
1 teaspoon **freshly ground black pepper**
½ teaspoon **dried Mexican oregano**
½ teaspoon **smoked paprika**
¼ teaspoon **ground cumin**
⅛ teaspoon **ground cloves**
2 tablespoons **sea salt**
2 pounds (910 g) **flap steak**
4 **spring onions** (can substitute 6 green onions), trimmed
1 cup (40 g) chopped **fresh cilantro**
½ large **white onion** (5¼ ounces/150 g), sliced
2 **serrano chiles**, sliced lengthwise

For serving:
Warm tortillas (preferably homemade; recipes on pages 46–51)
Salsa taquera (pages 193 and 197)

In a large bowl, add the orange juice, lime juice, oil, vinegar, Worcestershire sauce, garlic, and beer. Whisk to combine. Add the pepper, oregano, paprika, cumin, ground cloves, and salt, and whisk until the salt and spices have dissolved.

Pat the meat dry with paper towels. Using the palm of your hand against a flat surface, lightly smash the spring onions until a little moisture comes out. In a gallon-size resealable bag, add them along with the marinade, cilantro, onion, serranos, and the meat. Mix well, seal, and let sit in the refrigerator for at least 2 hours or overnight.

Remove the steaks from the refrigerator to allow them to reach room temperature before grilling, still in marinade, if possible. This should take at least 30 minutes.

Start a charcoal or gas grill. The gas should be set to high. If using a pellet grill, preheat your grill to 450°F (230°C) for at least 15 minutes. If using charcoal, the coals should be red but entirely covered with gray ash.

Remove the steaks from the marinade and put them on the grill directly over the fire. Close the lid and cook, turning once, about 4 to 5 minutes on each side. Transfer the meat to a cutting board and let rest for 5 minutes.

Slice the meat against the grain. Serve with warm tortillas and salsa.

Michelada Carne Asada

Serves 4

Fourth of July in Los Angeles is something that everyone must experience at least once in their lives. There are so many explosions in the sky and family carne asadas going on at once that the sky is one big puff of smoke. I usually host my family and, one time, I thought: *What if I added my family's michelada mix to my carne asada marinade?* The result was incredible. It tenderized the meat and added a savory and spicy juiciness that goes perfectly . . . with a michelada, of course! Our mix is inspired by the way micheladas are prepared in Oaxaca, which emphasizes sauces and dried chiles over a tomato cocktail mix. The longer the marinade, the better, but the steak also tastes great after just 30 minutes of marinating time.

½ tablespoon **garlic powder**

1 teaspoon **ground cumin**

2 tablespoons **sea salt**

2 teaspoons **freshly ground black pepper**

2 pounds (910 g) **flap steak**

½ cup (120 ml) **I Love Micheladas mix** (available online)

¼ cup (60 ml) **tomato juice**

¼ cup (60 ml) **orange juice**, freshly squeezed if in season

12 ounces (360 ml) **Mexican lager beer**

1 **jumbo shallot** (3¾ ounces/105 g), sliced

1 **orange**, sliced

For serving:

Warm tortillas (preferably homemade; recipes on pages 46–51)

Salsa of your choice (pages 184–211)

Whisk together the garlic powder, cumin, salt, and pepper in a small bowl. Pat the steak dry with paper towels, then sprinkle the rub evenly over both sides of the meat, gently patting to help it stick. Let sit for at least 10 minutes or up to 1 hour.

Meanwhile, in a large nonreactive bowl, combine the michelada mix, tomato juice, orange juice, and beer. Submerge the seasoned meat in the marinade and top with the shallot and orange slices. Put the bowl in the refrigerator and allow the meat to marinate for at least 4 hours or overnight.

Remove the meat from the refrigerator to allow it to reach room temperature before grilling, if possible.

Start a charcoal or gas grill. The gas should be set to high. If using a pellet grill, preheat your grill to 450°F (230°C) for at least 15 minutes. If using charcoal, the coals should be red but entirely covered with gray ash.

Remove the meat from the marinade and put it on the grill directly over the fire. Close the lid and cook, turning once, about 4 to 5 minutes on each side. Transfer the meat to a cutting board and let rest for 5 minutes.

Slice the meat against the grain. Serve with warm tortillas and salsa.

Carne Asada Enchilada

Serves 4

In Oaxaca, we rub a chile paste on meats like cecina, which is thinly sliced pork meant for grilling. This marinade is perfect for chile lovers who always add hot sauce to their food or find themselves always looking for or asking for some kind of salsa. It has a mild heat that gets unlocked when you add a little bit of lime juice.

8 **cloves garlic**, peeled
½ large **white onion** (5¼ ounces/150 g)
1 **chile manzano** (2¾ ounces/75 g), stems removed (can substitute 2 serranos)
4 **guajillo chiles**, stems and seeds removed
4 **pasilla chiles** (1¾ ounces/45 g), stems and seeds removed
1 cup (240 ml) **orange juice**, freshly squeezed if in season
½ cup (120 ml) **fresh lime juice**
½ cup (120 ml) **citrus vinegar** (can substitute seasoned rice wine vinegar)
1½ tablespoons **sherry**, preferably Tres Coronas
2 tablespoons **grapeseed oil**
1 tablespoon crushed **piloncillo** (Mexican unrefined brown sugar; can substitute dark brown sugar)
1 tablespoon **ground cumin**
2½ teaspoons **ground coriander**
2 tablespoons **sea salt**
2 pounds (910 g) **flap steak**
1 medium **white onion** (8¾ ounces/250 g), sliced
1 **orange**, sliced

For serving:
Warm tortillas (preferably homemade; recipes on pages 46–51)
Salsa of your choice (pages 184–211)

Start a charcoal or gas grill. The gas should be set to high. If using a pellet grill, preheat your grill to 450°F (230°C) for at least 15 minutes. If using charcoal, the coals should be red but entirely covered with gray ash.

Wrap the garlic in aluminum foil. Place the wrapped garlic, the onion, and chile manzano on the grill. Cover and cook until everything—except the garlic, which will be tender—is charred, about 15 minutes, turning once. Remove to a plate. Toast the guajillo and pasilla chiles over the grill until aromatic, about 1 minute per side. Remove to the plate.

In a high-speed blender, add the charred onion, garlic, and chiles along with the orange juice, lime juice, vinegar, sherry, oil, piloncillo, cumin, coriander, and salt. Blend until smooth.

Pat the meat dry with paper towels. Using a gallon-size resealable bag, add the marinade, the onion and orange slices, and the meat. Seal and let sit in the refrigerator for at least 2 hours or overnight.

Remove the steaks from the marinade and put them on the grill directly over the fire. Close the lid and cook, turning once, about 4 to 5 minutes on each side. Transfer the meat to a cutting board and let rest for 5 minutes.

Slice the meat against the grain. Serve with warm tortillas and salsa.

Arrachera Verde

Serves 4

Quick marinades can save your life at a carne asada. This one breaks down meat in about 30 minutes and is inspired by chimichurri—except much spicier. It's a great way to add some brightness to your carne asada.

1 cup (40 g) loosely packed **fresh basil** (leaves and tender stems)

½ cup (25 g) loosely packed **fresh mint** (leaves and tender stems)

½ cup (25 g) loosely packed **fresh parsley** (leaves and tender stems)

¼ cup **fresh oregano leaves**

2 **Fresno chiles**

3 large **cloves garlic**, peeled

Zest and juice of 1 **lemon** (about ¼ cup/60 ml)

¼ cup (60 ml) **olive oil**

1 teaspoon **citrus vinegar**

2 tablespoons **sea salt**

2 pounds (910 g) **flap steak**

For serving:

Warm tortillas (preferably homemade; recipes on pages 46–51)

Salsa de Piña Tatemada (page 195)

In a food processor, add the basil, mint, parsley, oregano, chiles, garlic, lemon zest and juice, olive oil, vinegar, and salt. Pulse until a smooth paste forms.

Pat the steak dry with paper towels and place in a large bowl. Rub the paste mixture all over the meat. Cover and refrigerate for at least 30 minutes or overnight.

Remove the meat from the refrigerator to allow it to reach room temperature before grilling, if possible.

Start a charcoal or gas grill. The gas should be set to high. If using a pellet grill, preheat your grill to 450°F (230°C) for at least 15 minutes. If using charcoal, the coals should be red but entirely covered with gray ash.

Remove the meat from the marinade and put it on the grill directly over the fire. Close the lid and cook, turning once, about 4 to 5 minutes on each side. Transfer the meat to a cutting board and let rest for 5 minutes.

Slice the meat against the grain. Serve with warm tortillas and the salsa.

Citrus and Spice Costillitas

Serves 4

This recipe is inspired by the iconic Mexican flavor combo found in so many candies and packaged marinade powders: dried chile and citrus. Now you can make your own. You can double or quadruple the yield and keep any leftover spice mix—before adding the juice—in a container with a tightly fitting lid, in your pantry, for later. Chile-citrus powder adds a punch of flavor to anything it touches, including potatoes, chicken, and pork.

1 teaspoon **guajillo chile powder**
1 teaspoon **smoked chipotle powder**
1 teaspoon **ground cumin**
½ teaspoon **onion powder**
½ teaspoon **garlic powder**
½ teaspoon **dried cilantro**
¼ teaspoon **dark brown sugar**
1 teaspoon **soy sauce**
Zest and juice of 1 **lime** (about 2 tablespoons)
Zest of ½ large **orange**
Juice of 2 large **oranges** (about ¾ cup/180 ml)
2 pounds (910 g) **flanken beef ribs**

For serving:
Warm tortillas (preferably homemade; recipes on pages 46–51)
Salsa of your choice (pages 184–211)

In a bowl, add the guajillo powder, chipotle powder, cumin, onion powder, garlic powder, dried cilantro, brown sugar, soy sauce, lime zest and juice, the orange zest, and the orange juice. Whisk to combine.

Pat the meat dry with paper towels. Using a gallon-size resealable bag, add the marinade and the meat. Seal and let sit in the refrigerator for at least 30 minutes or overnight.

Remove the steaks from the fridge to allow them to reach room temperature before grilling, if possible.

Start a charcoal or gas grill. The gas should be set to high. If using a pellet grill, preheat your grill to 450°F (230°C) for at least 15 minutes. If using charcoal, the coals should be red but entirely covered with gray ash.

Remove the steaks from the marinade and put them on the grill directly over the fire. Close the lid and cook, turning once, about 4 to 5 minutes on each side. Transfer the meat to a cutting board and let rest for 5 minutes.

Slice the meat against the grain. Serve with warm tortillas and salsa.

Rib Eye Para Taquear

Serves 4

Many would probably be surprised to find that most carne asada in Mexico is seasoned with just salt, especially in the northern states like Sonora and Nuevo León, where carne asada culture was born. You'll often see restaurants with the words "Grill," "Prime," and "Asadero" in their names, and the only thing on the menu are various cuts of carne asada. These two states consume the most beef per capita in all of Mexico, and they have adopted a more purist approach to carne asada, relying instead on the quality of the beef over a marinade for flavor. This rib eye proves that everything really is better when eaten over a tortilla. For this recipe, feel free to treat yourself to Prime-grade beef, Wagyu, Kobe, dry-aged beef, or any other highly marbled, aged piece of thick-cut beef.

---

3 pounds (1.4 kg) **rib eye** or **skirt steak** (arrachera), about 2 thick steaks
1½ tablespoons **sea salt**
8 **flour tortillas** (preferably homemade; recipe on page 46)

For the garnish:
Minced onion
Cilantro

For serving:
2 **limes**, sliced in half
1 cup (120 g) **Cucumber and Radish Taquero Salad** (page 167)
½ cup (120 ml) **Salsa Taquera en Molcajete** (page 193)

Start a charcoal or gas grill. The gas should be set to high. If using a pellet grill, preheat your grill to 450°F (230°C) for at least 15 minutes. If using charcoal, the coals should be red but entirely covered with gray ash.

Cut off a little piece of beef fat from a steak and, using a pair of tongs, rub the beef fat all over the grill to season the surface before grilling.

Season both sides of the steaks with salt. Let sit for 10 minutes, and then place it on the hot grill and cover. Let cook for 5 minutes. Uncover, flip to the other side, and let cook for another 3 minutes. The steaks are medium rare when their internal temperature reaches 130°F (54°C) on a meat thermometer. Remove the steaks from the grill and let rest on a cutting board for 5 minutes.

While the steaks are resting, place your flour tortillas on the grill to toast, about 1 minute per side. Set aside. Slice the steak against the grain into ½-inch (12 mm) pieces. Assemble the chopped steak over the tortillas, garnish each with a tablespoon of onion and cilantro, and serve with the limes, salad, and salsa. Enjoy.

Salsa Borracha Ribs

Serves 6

This is the kind of recipe that you purposely make at the end of an asada when everyone is already kind of full, just so you can hopefully have some leftovers. The meat absolutely falls apart and the sauciness of the dish lends itself perfectly to being tucked into a torta and devoured the next day.

For the rub:

2 tablespoons **sweet pimentón** (can substitute smoked paprika)

1½ tablespoons **garlic powder**

1 tablespoon **sea salt**

1 tablespoon **onion powder**

2½ teaspoons **ancho chile powder**

1 teaspoon **freshly ground black pepper**

½ teaspoon **dried oregano**

½ teaspoon **dried thyme**

2 racks **St. Louis–style pork ribs**, trimmed (5 to 7 pounds/2.3 to 3.2 kg)

For the sauce:

1¼ cups (300 ml) **tomato sauce**

1 (5-ounce/140 g) can **chipotle in adobo** (4 to 5 chiles)

1 medium **white onion** (10½ ounces/300 g), ¾ quartered and ¼ minced

2 **cloves garlic**, minced

1 tablespoon **olive oil**

½ cup (120 ml) **distilled white vinegar**

⅓ cup (75 ml) **Worcestershire sauce**

2 tablespoons **dark brown sugar**

2 tablespoons **Tabasco hot sauce**

1 tablespoon **tomato paste**

1 tablespoon **sea salt**

12 ounces (360 ml) **dark Mexican beer**

Make the rub: In a small bowl, whisk together all the pimentón, garlic powder, salt, onion powder, ancho chile powder, pepper, oregano, and thyme.

Place the ribs in a shallow pan and generously rub the spice mix all over the racks of ribs, on both sides. Cover and refrigerate for 1 hour.

While the ribs are marinating, make the sauce: In a blender, add the tomato sauce, chipotle chiles including some of the sauce, the onion quarters, and the garlic. Blend until smooth and set aside.

Heat the olive oil in a saucepan over medium heat. Once the oil is hot, add the minced onion and stir until translucent and fragrant, about 5 minutes. Carefully add the blended tomato sauce. Bring the sauce to a boil over medium heat and cook until it has reduced by a third, about 10 minutes. Add the vinegar, Worcestershire sauce, brown sugar, Tabasco, tomato paste, and salt and stir to combine. Lower the heat and continue to cook for another 20 minutes, until the sauce has thickened. Remove from the heat and allow to cool.

Preheat your grill to 275°F (135°C) if using a pellet grill. If you don't have a pellet smoker, you may use your oven for this step.

On a work surface, spread out 2 large sheets of aluminum foil on top of each other (big enough to wrap each of the racks individually). Working one at a time, remove a rack of ribs from the fridge and place it on top of a piece of foil. Pour about half of the cooled sauce over the top and wrap the ribs in the foil, pleating the edges so the package seals well. Repeat with the second rack.

continued

Place the ribs in the middle of your preheated grill or oven, meat side up, and cook for 3 hours. After 3 hours, carefully uncover the ribs. Reserve 1 cup (240 ml) of sauce in a serving bowl for dipping later. Liberally brush the ribs with the rest of the sauce. Cover the ribs again and allow to cook for 1 more hour.

Remove the ribs and prepare your grill for hot direct cooking. Make sure the grates are clean.

If using a pellet grill, raise to high heat and crisp your ribs for about 4 minutes on each side, until the ribs are fall-apart tender and really saucy. If using a pellet grill, remove the ribs, carefully remove the grill grate using two tongs and grilling gloves, and add more charcoal until you reach a higher temperature, and place the ribs back on the grill to crisp up then.

Once the ribs are crispy, using either two spatulas or a spatula and tongs, remove the ribs to a platter and serve right away, with the leftover sauce on the side. The ribs may be so tender, that they will shred when you try to serve yourself!

Pollo Yucateco Asado

Serves 6

Pollo asado is an institution on the streets of L.A. You'll smell it immediately on random intersections around the city and in front of Mexican and Central American markets on weekends. The enchanting smell of charcoal-grilled chicken has a way of seeping into your car when you're stuck at a long red light, making you really hungry. Most people will offer pollo asado as an option for their guests when hosting a carne asada. You can use chicken breast, if you prefer.

¼ teaspoon **cumin seeds**
1 **whole clove**
1 **whole allspice berry**
1½ teaspoons **dried Mexican oregano**
2½ tablespoons **ground achiote**
1½ tablespoons **sea salt**
1½ teaspoons **ground white pepper**
1½ teaspoons **garlic powder**
¼ cup (120 ml) **distilled white vinegar**
Juice of one **orange**, about ⅓ cup (75 ml) fresh orange juice + half an orange, silced with peel on
2 tablespoons **olive oil**
3 pounds (1.3 kg) **bone-in chicken thighs**

For serving:
Arroz blanco (page 145)
Frijoles negros (page 135)
Warm tortillas (preferably homemade; recipes on pages 46–51)
Salsa de Piña Tatemada (page 195)

In a cast-iron skillet over medium heat, add the cumin seeds, clove, allspice, and oregano. Toast for about 2 minutes or until the spices are aromatic. Grind everything in a molcajete or spice grinder until finely ground.

In a medium bowl, whisk together the toasted ground spices, the achiote, salt, white pepper, garlic powder, vinegar, orange juice, and olive oil until well combined.

Pat the chicken dry with paper towels. Using a gallon-size resealable bag, add the marinade, the orange slices, and the chicken. Seal and let sit in the refrigerator for at least 30 minutes but preferably overnight.

Before grilling, remove the chicken thighs in their marinade from the fridge to allow them to return to room temperature.

Start a charcoal or gas grill. The gas should be set to high. If using a pellet grill, preheat your grill to 450°F (230°C) for at least 15 minutes. If using charcoal, the coals should be red but entirely covered with gray ash.

Remove the chicken thighs from the marinade while reserving a few orange slices to grill as well, and put them on the grill directly over the high fire, skin side up. Close the lid and cook, turning once, for about 15 minutes on each side. The chicken is cooked when its internal temperature reaches 175°F (79°C) on a meat thermometer. Transfer the meat to a cutting board and let rest for 5 minutes.

Serve the chicken with arroz blanco, frijoles negros, tortillas, and salsa.

Citrus and Oregano Pollo Asado

Serves 4

Citrus and oregano make this grilled chicken taste sophisticated. It is inspired by my mom's traditional pollo en oregano, which is usually fried. (You can find that recipe in our first cookbook *Oaxaca: Home Cooking from the Heart of Mexico.*)

1½ tablespoons **dried oregano**
¼ teaspoon **cumin seeds**
¼ teaspoon **whole black peppercorns** (about 12 peppercorns)
1 head **garlic** (1¼ ounces/35 g), cloves separated, peeled, and minced
2 tablespoons **olive oil**
1½ tablespoons **sea salt**
Juice of 2 **lemons** (about ½ cup/120 ml)
3 pounds (1.3 kg) **bone-in chicken thighs**

In a cast-iron skillet over medium heat, toast the oregano, cumin seeds, and peppercorns for about 3 minutes, until the spices are aromatic. Grind everything in a molcajete or spice grinder until finely ground.

In a medium bowl, whisk together the toasted ground spices, garlic, oil, salt, and lemon juice.

Pat the chicken dry with paper towels. Using a gallon-size resealable bag, add the marinade and the chicken. Seal and let sit in the refrigerator for at least 30 minutes but preferably overnight.

Remove the chicken thighs in their marinade from the fridge to allow them to reach room temperature.

Start a charcoal or gas grill. The gas should be set to high. If using a pellet grill, preheat your grill to 450°F (230°C) for at least 15 minutes. If using charcoal, the coals should be red but entirely covered with gray ash.

Remove the chicken thighs from the marinade and put them on the grill directly over the high fire, skin side up. Close the lid and cook, turning once, about 15 minutes on each side. The chicken is cooked when its internal temperature reaches 175°F (79°C) on a meat thermometer. Transfer the meat to a cutting board and let rest for 5 minutes before serving.

Pollo in Guajillo

Serves 4

This grilled chicken has gotten me through so many long days working at Guelaguetza. There were times when I ate it for lunch every day, sometimes with a big salad, sometimes with homestyle french fries, or with rice, beans, and tortillas. It tastes great any way you eat it and it reheats beautifully. This is a solid recipe to make on a Sunday and eat throughout the week. I purposely did not soak the chiles, in order to create a rustic marinade that has more texture; the flavor of burnt chile once it is grilled makes this chicken recipe stand out.

---

12 **guajillo chiles** (1¾ ounces/50 g), stems and seeds removed
½ large **white onion** (5¼ ounces/150 g), roughly chopped
8 **cloves garlic**, peeled
¼ teaspoon **black peppercorns** (about 12 peppercorns)
1 **whole clove**
1 tablespoon **dried Mexican oregano**
2 tablespoons **grapeseed oil**
¼ cup (60 ml) **orange juice**
2 tablespoons **seasoned rice vinegar**
2 tablespoons **fresh lime juice**
¼ teaspoon **ground cinnamon**
1½ tablespoons **sea salt**
2 pounds (910 g) **bone-in chicken thighs**

In a cast-iron skillet over medium heat, lightly toast the chiles, about 2 to 3 minutes on each side. Remove from the skillet and set aside.

In the same skillet, add the onion and garlic, turning once or twice until they are lightly charred, about 10 minutes. Remove from the skillet and set aside.

Add the peppercorns, clove, and dried oregano to the pan and lightly toast until they are aromatic, about 2 minutes. Transfer the toasted spices and oregano to a molcajete or spice grinder and grind until finely ground.

In a high-performance blender or food processor, add the toasted chiles, onion, garlic, ground spices and oregano, oil, orange juice, rice vinegar, lime juice, cinnamon, and salt. Blend until most of the chiles have come apart.

Pat the chicken dry with paper towels. Using a gallon-size resealable bag, add the marinade and the chicken. Seal and let sit in the refrigerator for at least 30 minutes or overnight.

Remove the chicken thighs in their marinade from the fridge to allow them to reach room temperature before grilling.

Start a charcoal or gas grill. The gas should be set to high. If using a pellet grill, preheat your grill to 450°F (230°C) for at least 15 minutes. If using charcoal, the coals should be red but entirely covered with gray ash.

Remove the chicken from the marinade and put them on the grill directly over the medium fire, skin side up. Close the lid and cook, turning once, about 15 minutes on each side. The chicken is cooked when its internal temperature reaches 175°F (79°C) on a meat thermometer. Transfer the meat to a cutting board and let rest for 5 minutes.

Cecina Oaxaqueña

Serves 4 to 6

This is as close as you get to carne asada in Oaxaca. You'll find cecina on menus on top of enfrijoladas, on your tlayudas (page 51), and just served on a plate. The dried chiles not only add an addictive flavor, but a beautiful color as well that lends itself to perfect grill marks.

20 **guajillo chiles** (2½ ounces/70 g), stems and seeds removed
8 **cloves garlic**, peeled
¾ tablespoon **dried oregano**
1 teaspoon **dried thyme**
¼ teaspoon **cumin seeds**
4 **whole cloves**
2 **whole allspice berries**
½ large **white onion** (5¼ ounces/150 g), roughly chopped
¼ cup (120 ml) **apple cider vinegar**
2 tablespoons **grapeseed oil**
3 tablespoons **sea salt**
1 teaspoon **sugar**
¼ teaspoon **ground cinnamon**
1 **bay leaf**
2 pounds (910 g) thinly sliced **pork loin cutlets**

Bring a pot of water to a boil. Remove from the heat, submerge the chiles in the water, and cover. Leave for 15 minutes or until the chiles are very tender. Drain, reserving ½ cup (120 ml) of the soaking liquid.

On a comal or skillet over medium heat, place the garlic and toast until aromatic and the edges are lightly charred. In a molcajete or spice grinder, grind the oregano, thyme, cumin seeds, cloves, and allspice berries.

Put the softened chiles with the reserved soaking water into a blender, along with the ground spice mixture, garlic, onion, vinegar, oil, salt, sugar, cinnamon, and bay leaf. Blend until smooth. Set aside.

One at a time, place each slice of cutlet between two sheets of parchment paper on a butcher block. Using a meat mallet, pound the meat until it is as thin as possible, almost as thin as sliced ham, without the meat breaking apart.

Using a gallon-size resealable bag, add the marinade and the pounded cutlets. Seal and let sit in the refrigerator for at least 30 minutes or overnight.

Remove the cutlets in their marinade from the refrigerator to allow them to reach room temperature before grilling.

Start a charcoal or gas grill. The gas should be set to high. If using a pellet grill, preheat your grill to 450°F (230°C) for at least 15 minutes. If using charcoal, the coals should be red but entirely covered with gray ash.

Using a pair of kitchen tongs, Remove the pork slices from the marinade and put them on the grill directly over the high fire. Close the lid and cook, turning once, about 3 to 5 minutes on each side. Transfer the meat to a cutting board and let rest for 5 minutes.

Pibil-Style Pork Chops

Serves 6 to 8

Cochinita pibil is a religion for some people, especially in Yucatán where the dish originated. Like many other meat dishes, it's all about the marinade. This is our quick-grilling tribute to the iconic dish using pork chops instead of beef. You'll find achiote paste, which adds a brilliant color and uniquely spiced flavor, in Mexican markets, and it is also available online.

1 head **garlic** (1¼ ounces/35 g), cloves separated, peeled, and minced

½ teaspoon **whole allspice berries**

¼ teaspoon **whole black peppercorns**

2 tablespoons **sea salt**

4 pounds (1.8 kg) **bone-in pork chops**, about ¼ inch (6 mm) thick

6 ounces (170 g) **achiote paste**

1 large **white onion** (10½ ounces/300 g)

1¾ cups (420 ml) **orange juice**, freshly squeezed if in season

1 tablespoon **fresh lime juice**

¼ cup (60 ml) **apple cider vinegar**

1 tablespoon **grapeseed oil**

1 teaspoon **dried oregano**

½ teaspoon **ground cumin**

1¼-inch (3 cm) piece **cinnamon stick**

For serving:

Pickled Red Onions (page 159)

Salsa of your choice (pages 184–211)

Tortillas (preferably homemade; recipes on pages 46–51)

In a mortar and pestle, grind the garlic, allspice, peppercorns, and salt until it has reached a paste consistency. Alternatively, you could grind the spices in the mortar separately and then pulse the garlic and ground spices in a mini food processor to form the paste.

Put the pork chops in a large rectangular container and generously and evenly rub the paste all over the chops. Cover and allow the meat to marinate in the refrigerator for 1 hour.

Meanwhile, in a high-performance blender or food processor, add the achiote paste, onion, orange juice, lime juice, vinegar, oil, oregano, cumin, and piece of cinnamon stick. Blend until smooth. Pour the blended mixture on top of the marinated pork chops and return to the fridge for at least 1 more hour or overnight.

Remove the pork chops in their marinade from the fridge to allow them to reach room temperature before grilling.

Start a charcoal or gas grill. The gas should be set to high. If using a pellet grill, preheat your grill to 450°F (230°C) for at least 15 minutes. If using charcoal, the coals should be red but entirely covered with gray ash.

Remove the pork chops from the marinade and put them on the grill directly over the high fire. Close the lid and cook, turning once, for about 10 minutes total. The pork chops are done when their internal temperature reaches 145°F (62°C) on a meat thermometer. Transfer the meat to a cutting board and let rest for 5 minutes.

Slice the pork chops and serve with pickled onions, salsa, and tortillas.

Tacos de Lengua Asada

Serves 4

When properly cooked, the flavor and texture of lengua is incredibly tender and buttery. We're pretty sure that most people would think it was straight-up carne asada if you didn't tell them it was actually beef tongue. Grilling it unlocks its meaty qualities even more.

1 **beef tongue** (1½ to 2 pounds/680 to 910 g)
1 large **white onion** (10½ ounces/300 g), quartered
1 head **garlic** (1 ounce /30 g), cut in half, not peeled
10 **black peppercorns**
4 **bay leaves**
1 tablespoon **dried oregano**
1 tablespoon **dried marjoram**
4 sprigs **thyme**
1 sprig **mint**
2 tablespoons **sea salt**, plus more as needed
¼ cup (60 ml) **grapeseed oil**
Freshly ground black pepper

For serving:
Lime wedges
Finishing sea salt
Tortillas (preferably homemade; recipes on pages 46–51)
Cucumber and Radish Taquero Salad (page 167)
Salsa Frita Verde (page 199)

In a heavy-bottomed pot, add 3 quarts (3 L) water, the tongue, onion, garlic, peppercorns, bay leaves, oregano, marjoram, thyme, mint, and salt and bring to a boil. When the water starts to boil, reduce the heat to low and simmer, covered, for about 3 hours. Add more hot water if needed to keep all the ingredients covered. The tongue is ready when the thickest part is tender enough that it has little to no resistance when you touch it.

Using kitchen tongs, remove the tongue from the broth and allow it to cool for about 10 minutes, just until cool enough to touch. Carefully remove the outer layer of skin and membrane and discard it. It should come off with ease if the tongue is still warm.

Let cool to room temperature and slice the tongue into ½-inch-thick (12 mm) slices. Brush each slice with the oil and season generously with salt and pepper on both sides.

Start a charcoal or gas grill. The gas should be set to high. If using a pellet grill, preheat your grill to 450°F (230°C) for at least 15 minutes. If using charcoal, the coals should be red but entirely covered with gray ash.

Place the slices of tongue on the grill, directly over the high fire. Close the lid and cook, turning once, for about 5 minutes on each side, until they get nice and crispy. Transfer the meat to a cutting board and let rest for 5 minutes. Chop into cubes and finish with a squeeze of lime and finishing salt.

Serve in tacos with the salad and salsa.

Smoked Lamb Barbacoa

Serves 8 to 10

This variation is inspired by the barbacoa de borrego that my family and I grew up eating in Tlacolula's famous Sunday *tianguis* (open-air market) that takes place every Sunday, specifically the booth owned by Doña Adolfa. Slowly smoking the chile- and spice-rubbed lamb in banana leaves adds an incredible depth of flavor.

12 **guajillo chiles** (2½ ounces/70 g), stems and seeds removed
2 teaspoons **cumin seeds**
1 teaspoon **anise seeds**
4 tablespoons (9 g) **dried Mexican oregano**
1 inch (2.5 cm) piece **cinnamon stick**
½ teaspoon **dried thyme**
4 **whole cloves**
4 **whole black peppercorns**
4 **bay leaves**
2 **whole allspice berries**
1 head **garlic** (1⅓ ounces/35 g), cloves separated and peeled
2 medium **white onions** (1¼ pounds/600 g), quartered
3 tablespoons **sea salt**
1 tablespoon **red wine vinegar**
3 pounds (1.4 kg) **lamb shoulder roast**
8 ounces (225 g) **banana leaves**, washed and soaked
¼ cup (60 ml) **bone broth**

For serving:
Tortillas (preferably homemade; recipes on pages 46–51)
"Con Todo" Topping (page 212)
Finishing sea salt
Lime wedges

Bring a pot of water to boil. Remove from the heat, submerge the chiles, and cover. Leave for 15 minutes or until the chiles are very tender. Drain, reserving ½ cup (120 ml) of the soaking liquid.

In a large cast-iron skillet over medium-low heat, toast the cumin seeds, anise seeds, oregano, cinnamon stick, thyme, cloves, peppercorns, bay leaves, and allspice for about 7 minutes, until evenly toasted.

While the spices are toasting, lightly char the garlic and onion in a preheated broiler, for about 6 minutes or until the edges of the onion are nicely charred.

In a molcajete or spice grinder, grind the toasted spices.

In a blender, combine the softened chiles, the garlic, onion, toasted spices, salt, and vinegar. Blend until you have a fine and smooth paste.

Reserve 1 cup (240 ml) of the marinade to use later. Put the lamb in a large bowl and run the remaining marinade on all sides. Cover and refrigerate for at least 2 hours or overnight. Remove the lamb shoulder from the refrigerator 30 minutes before cooking, so it can come to room temperature.

When ready to cook, preheat a pellet grill to 375°F (190°C) with the lid closed, for 15 minutes. Or you can use your oven instead.

Remove the lamb from the bowl and place it in a dutch oven lined with banana leaves. Fold the banana leaves over the lamb to tightly seal and cover the pot. Cook the lamb for 2 hours.

continued

After 2 hours, carefully remove the banana leaves from the pot using kitchen tongs. Pour the 1 cup (240 ml) reserved marinade and the bone broth on top of the lamb shoulder. Cover the pot and cook for another 2 hours. Remove the cover and continue cooking the lamb until it is browned and tender, about 1 more hour, occasionally spooning the juices on top.

Remove the lamb from the grill or oven and allow it to rest for at least 20 minutes. Tear the meat apart using two forks, and combine it with the remaining liquid in the bottom of the pan. Serve with tortillas, "con todo" topping, finishing salt, and lime wedges.

L.A. Streets Dog

Makes 4 hot dogs

In Los Angeles, asada tacos and bacon-wrapped hot dogs exist side by side during the late hours to sober you up after a wild night out. They satisfy your cravings when everything else is closed or seemingly too far away and you just need a little something before you go to sleep. This is my tribute to that L.A. street classic. For the full effect, buy a squeeze bottle to fill with mayonnaise and squiggle it over the hot dog, along with the ketchup and mustard. The trick with cooking bacon-wrapped hot dogs on the grill is to keep them covered and not mess with them as they cook to control any flare-ups caused by dripping bacon fat.

2 tablespoons **grapeseed oil**, plus more for greasing the grill

4 **hot dogs**

4 slices **bacon** (2 ounces/60 g)

½ large **white onion** (5¼ ounces/150 g), sliced crosswise into 2 thick pieces

2 large **red bell peppers**

2 large **jalapeños**

4 **hot dog buns**

Mayonnaise

Ketchup

Mustard

Preheat your grill to 375°F (190°C) if using a pellet grill, to low heat if using gas, or for indirect cooking if using charcoal, with the lid closed, for 15 minutes. Place a paper towel on the end of your bottle of grapeseed oil and flip it so that the paper towel absorbs a little bit of oil. Using tongs, carefully apply the oiled end of the paper towel all over the grill to make sure the bacon does not stick while cooking.

Cut a couple slits into each hot dog so they won't burst while grilling. Carefully wrap each one with bacon, using a toothpick to secure the bacon to the hot dog. Try to get it as tightly wound as you can. In a bowl, carefully toss the onions with the oil. Make sure to keep the large pieces intact.

Carefully place each hot dog on the grill, along with the whole bell peppers, the jalapeños, and the onion. Cover the grill and let cook. After 15 minutes, flip the hot dogs and vegetables. After another 15 minutes, the hot dogs should be nicely grilled and the bacon a little crispy. Remove the hot dogs and vegetables from the grill.

When the grilled bell peppers and jalapeños have cooled enough to handle, slice them in half and remove the seeds. Cut them into strips.

Add the opened hot dog buns to the grill and toast them until lightly browned. To assemble the hot dogs, place them in the buns and layer each one with the bell peppers, jalapeños, and onion. Drizzle with as much mayonnaise, ketchup, and mustard as you like and eat!

Seafood

The term *asada* just means grilled. Cooking whole fish and seafood on the grill provides many of the same thrills as grilling meat. You can create all those smoky, juicy, charred, and delicious flavors and textures that you love about an asada on seafood, too. Whether you've been trying to eat less meat and add more seafood into your diet or you just want to have some options from the sea at your next asada for people who don't eat meat (or who love seafood), learning how to cook fish over an open fire is exhilarating and extremely rewarding.

LOS

MARI
SCOS

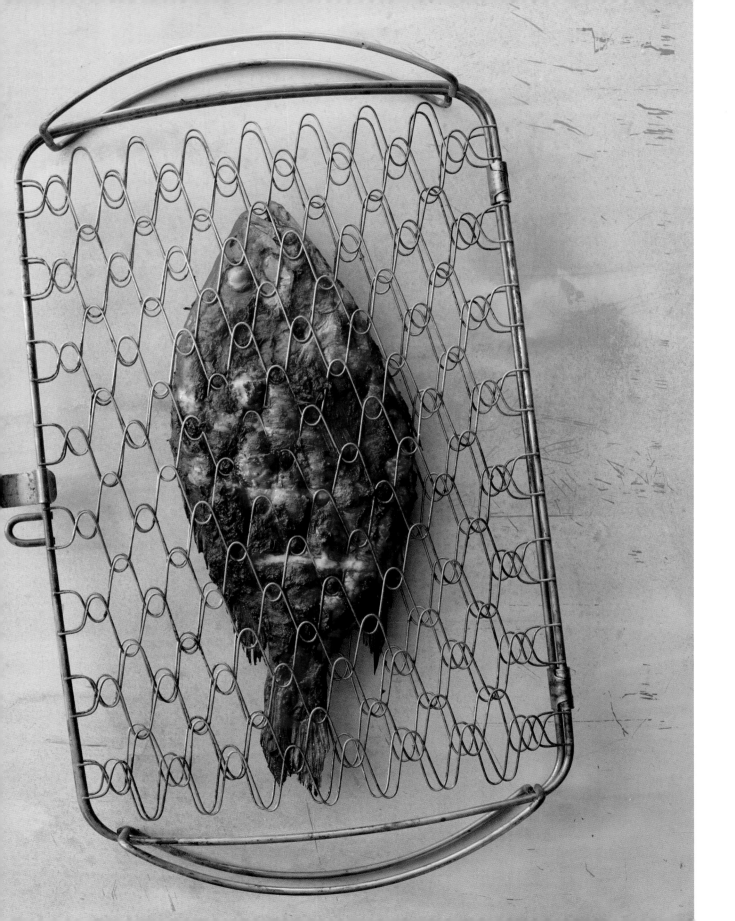

Four Chile Snapper

Serves 4 to 6

I grew up going to Huatulco with my father. Not to relax all day on the beach, but to keep him company while he sold his mezcal along the coast. After a long day of work, he always took us out to eat a grilled fish like this one as a sign of love after the long car ride from the city to the beach.

2 **dried morita chiles**
1 **ancho chile**, seeds removed
1 **dried guajillo chile**, seeds removed
1 **pasilla chile**, seeds removed
2 medium to large **whole red snappers** (2 to 3 pounds [910 g to 1.4 kg] each), scaled
4 medium **plum tomatoes** (1¼ ounces/565 g), cored
¼ medium **white onion** (2 ounces/55 g)
5 **cloves garlic**, peeled
2 **whole cloves**
½ cup (120 ml) **olive oil**
2 tablespoons **orange juice**, freshly squeezed if in season
1 tablespoon **fresh lime juice**
¼ teaspoon **ground cumin**
¼ teaspoon **dried Mexican oregano**
1 tablespoon **sea salt**

For serving:
Lime wedges
Finishing salt
Arroz Verde (page 142)

Bring 2 cups (480 ml) water to a boil. Remove from the heat, then add all of the chiles and soak them for about 10 minutes, covered, until they have softened. Meanwhile, pat the fish dry with paper towels and, with a small knife, gently slash the skin of each fish, about ¼ inch (6 mm) deep on a diagonal, three to four times on each side of the fish.

Once the chiles have softened, put them in a food processor and add the tomatoes, onion, garlic, cloves, olive oil, orange juice, lime juice, cumin, oregano, and salt. Blend until smooth.

Generously rub the marinade all over the fish, including inside the slashes. Place the fish in a large container and allow it to marinate in refrigerator for 1 hour.

Start a charcoal or gas grill. The gas should be set to medium. If using a pellet grill, preheat your grill to 425°F (220°C) for at least 15 minutes. If using charcoal, the coals should be red but entirely covered with gray ash.

With the help of a grilling basket, place the snapper on the grill. Close the grill's lid and cook for about 30 minutes, flipping once, until the fish flakes easily. Transfer the fish to a cutting board and let rest for 5 minutes. Serve with lime wedges, finishing salt, and the rice.

Grilled Snapper al Mojo de Ajo

Serves 4 to 6

Al mojo de ajo means "dipped in garlic" and it is one of Mexico's most popular techniques for cooking seafood. In practically every Mexican restaurant in the United States that has that iconic "Mexican and Seafood" neon sign, you will find al mojo on the menu. It is equally delicious on fish, shrimp, and octopus. This is our grilled version of the classic.

Sea salt
5 **whole allspice berries**
3 **whole black peppercorns**
½ large **shallot** (¾ ounce/21 g), sliced
10 **cloves garlic**, peeled
2 tablespoons **fresh lime juice**
1 tablespoon **fresh lemon juice**
2 tablespoons **grapeseed oil**
2 medium to large **whole red snappers** (2 to 3 pounds [910 g to 1.3 kg] each), scaled
2 **lemons**, sliced
1 bunch **fresh parsley**
1 bunch **fresh marjoram**

For serving:
Lime wedges
Finishing salt
Arroz Verde (page 142)

In a mortar and pestle, grind the salt, allspice, and peppercorns. Add the shallot and continue to grind until they dissolve and a paste forms. Add the garlic, a couple cloves at a time, and continue to grind until a paste forms. Add the lime juice, lemon juice, and oil. Mix everything together and set aside.

Pat the fish dry with paper towels and, with a small knife, gently slash the skin of each fish, about ¼ inch (6 mm) deep on a diagonal, three to four times on each side of the fish.

Generously rub the marinade all over the fish, including inside the slashes. Stuff the fish with the lemon slices, parsley, and marjoram. Place the fish in a large container and allow it to marinate in refrigerator for 1 hour.

Start a charcoal or gas grill. The gas should be set to medium. If using a pellet grill, preheat your grill to 425°F (220°C) for at least 15 minutes. If using charcoal, the coals should be red but entirely covered with gray ash.

With the help of a grilling basket, place the snapper on the grill. Close the grill's lid and cook for about 20 minutes, flipping the fish once. Transfer the fish to a cutting board and let it rest for 5 minutes. Serve with lime wedges, finishing salt, and the rice.

Peel 'n' Eat Guajillo Prawns

Serves 4

In Oaxaca, we get down and messy with our food. There is absolutely no shame in voraciously eating with our hands. Sometimes, like with this dish, it is absolutely necessary. Dare I say eating with our hands makes food taste even better? Fish sauce, traditionally used in southeast Asian cooking, is our secret ingredient in this recipe. It contributes such an amazing savoriness to anything you use it in.

2 **guajillo chiles**, stems and seeds removed
5 **chiles de árbol**, stems removed
9 **cloves garlic**, peeled
4 tablespoons (½ stick/55 g) **unsalted butter**
1 tablespoon **fish sauce**
1 tablespoon **fresh lime juice**
2 pounds (910 g) **extra-large shrimp** (about 16 to 20 per pound), shells on, rinsed and patted dry

For the garnishes:
Lime wedges
Finishing salt

In a cast-iron skillet over medium heat, toast the dried chiles until aromatic, about 3 minutes.

In a high-performance blender or a food processor, add the garlic, toasted chiles, butter, fish sauce, and lime juice. Puree until a smooth paste forms. Set aside.

Pat the shrimp dry with paper towels. Put the shrimp in a bowl, add the chile mixture, and toss to coat. Allow to marinate at room temperature for 25 minutes.

Start a charcoal or gas grill. The gas should be set to medium. If using a pellet grill, preheat your grill to 375°F (190°C) for at least 15 minutes. If using charcoal, the coals should be red but entirely covered with gray ash.

Place the shrimp on the grill directly over the medium fire. Close the lid and cook for about 10 minutes, flipping once. Serve with lime wedges and finishing salt.

Camarones a la Diabla Asados

Serves 4 to 6

Camarones a la diabla translates literally to "shrimp, the devil's way." It is a figure of speech referring to the fiery level of spiciness in the sweet and salty sauce the shrimp is flavored with. For our grilled variation, we put it on skewers.

3 tablespoons **grapeseed oil**
4 **cloves garlic**, peeled
½ large **white onion** (5¼ ounces/150 g), sliced
3 **whole allspice berries**
2 **ancho chiles**, seeds and stems removed
4 **guajillo chiles**, seeds and stems removed
4 **chiles de árbol**, stems removed
½ cup (120 ml) **tomato sauce**
2 tablespoons **fish sauce**
1 cup (240) **orange juice**, freshly squeezed if
    in season
4 **chipotles en adobo**, plus 1 tablespoon of sauce
    (3 ounces/80 g)
¼ cup (60 ml) **olive oil**
1 tablespoon **sea salt**, plus more as needed
2 pounds (910 g) **extra-large shrimp** (about 16
    to 20 per pound), peeled, deveined, rinsed,
    and patted dry

For serving:
Lime slices
Chopped fresh parsley
Arroz Blanco (page 145)

Heat the grapeseed oil in a large cast-iron skillet over medium-low heat. When hot, add the garlic, onions, allspice, and the anchos, guajillos, and árbol chiles. Cook and stir until the onions are translucent and the chiles are aromatic, about 10 minutes. Stir in the tomato sauce, fish sauce, and ¼ cup (60 ml) water. Increase the heat and allow the chile mixture to come to a soft boil. Remove from the heat, cover, and allow to rest for 10 minutes, until the chiles have softened.

In a blender, add the cooked chile mixture, orange juice, chipotles, olive oil, and salt. Blend until smooth. Taste for seasoning and add more salt as needed. Allow to cool.

Reserve ¼ cup (60 ml) of the chile sauce. In a bowl, toss the shrimp with the rest of the cooled sauce to combine well. Let marinate at room temperature for 15 minutes.

Start a charcoal or gas grill. The gas should be set to medium. If using a pellet grill, preheat your grill to 375°F (190°C) for at least 15 minutes. If using charcoal, the coals should be red but entirely covered with gray ash.

Divide the shrimp among 4 to 6 skewers and place them on the grill, directly over the medium fire. Close the lid and cook for about 8 minutes, flipping once and brushing with the reserved sauce, until the shrimp are firm and pink.

Serve with lime slices, fresh parsley, and the arroz blanco.

116

Aguachile Rojo

Serves 4

Not all dishes at a carne asada have to be grilled. Dishes like this aguachile provide a much-appreciated, refreshing contrast to all the grilled meat. Aguachile should always taste like its name makes it out to be: "fire water." This dish packs a punch of acid and heat, and prepares your appetite for the rest of the carne asada feasting to come.

2 pounds (910 g) **large shrimp** (about 15 to 17 per pound), peeled, deveined, rinsed, and patted dry

Juice of 12 **limes**, preferably key limes (about 1½ cups/360 ml)

4 red **Fresno chiles** (1¼ ounces/30 g), stems removed

1 to 2 **habanero chiles**, stems removed

2 tablespoons **olive oil**

½ teaspoon **sea salt**, plus more as needed

Freshly ground black pepper

1 cup (135 g) peeled and thinly sliced **English cucumber**

½ cup (65 g) thinly sliced **red onion**

2 tablespoons chopped **fresh cilantro**

For serving:

Tostadas (preferably homemade; recipe on page 52)

Lime slices

Chopped **fresh parsley**

Using a small, sharp knife, butterfly the shrimp by slicing almost all the way through the back side of each one. This will help the shrimp lay more flat while marinating and cooking.

Place the shrimp in a shallow glass dish. Pour three-fourths of the key lime juice (about 1 cup/240 ml) over the top, making sure the shrimp is covered. Cover the dish and chill in the refrigerator for about 15 minutes while you prep the rest of the ingredients.

In a blender, add the Fresno and habanero chiles, the juice of the remaining one-fourth key lime juice (about ½ cup/120 ml), the olive oil, and the salt. Blend until smooth. Taste for salt and adjust as needed.

Remove the shrimp from the refrigerator and pour the chile and lime dressing over the top, making sure it's mixed in with the shrimp evenly. Season with pepper. Layer the cucumbers, onions, and cilantro over the top. Chill for another 15 minutes or so.

Make sure the shrimp has been chilling in the fridge for at least 30 minutes before mixing it all together and serving with tostadas, lime slices, and chopped parsley.

Cóctel de Camarón Asado

Serves 8

A traditional cóctel de camarón is already a perfect food, but if you want to shake things up a bit, grilling the shrimp instead of poaching it in liquid adds an enticing smokiness. Using orange-flavored soda adds a sweet and tart flavor. It is actually one of those old-school "secret" ingredients used in shrimp cocktails usually served in the inland regions of Mexico.

1 tablespoon plus ½ teaspoon **sea salt**

2 teaspoons **ancho chile powder**

3 tablespoons **olive oil**

14 tablespoons (210 ml) **fresh lime juice**

3 pounds (1.35 kg) **large shrimp** (about 15 to 17 per pound), peeled, deveined, rinsed, and patted dry

1¾ cups (420 ml) **ketchup**

1 cup (240 ml) **orange soda**

3 **chipotles en adobo**, with 1 tablespoon sauce (2½ ounces/70 g)

¼ teaspoon **Maggi Seasoning sauce**

1 teaspoon **Worcestershire sauce**

2 teaspoons **fish sauce**

½ cup (20 g) finely chopped **fresh cilantro**

1 cup (130 g) chopped **red onion**

2 **Persian cucumbers**, finely chopped

2 medium **avocados**, pitted, cubed, and peeled

Saltine crackers, for serving

In a large bowl, mix 1 tablespoon of the salt, the ancho chile powder, 1 tablespoon of the olive oil, and 2 tablespoons of the lime juice. Add the shrimp and toss to combine.

Preheat your grill to 425°F (220°C) if using a pellet grill, to high heat if using gas, or for direct cooking if using charcoal, with the lid closed, for 15 minutes.

Place the marinated shrimp on skewers and place them on the grill, directly over the high fire. Close the lid and cook for about 8 minutes, flipping once, until the shrimp are firm and have turned pink. Remove from the grill and allow to cool.

In a blender, combine the ketchup, the remaining ¾ cup (180 ml) lime juice, the soda, chipotles, the remaining 2 tablespoons olive oil, the Maggi Seasoning, Worcestershire sauce, fish sauce, 1 cup (240 ml) water, and the remaining ½ teaspoon salt. Blend until smooth and transfer to a large bowl. Add the grilled shrimp, cilantro, chopped onion, and cucumbers to the bowl and stir to combine.

Top the shrimp cocktail with the avocados, divide among 8 cocktail glasses, and serve with saltine crackers.

Puerto Escondido–Style Fish and Shrimp Ceviche Tostadas

Serves 4 to 6

On really hot days, ceviche is the perfect thing to eat. There is no reason to feel overwhelmed when it comes to handling raw seafood. Contrary to popular belief, ceviche is not actually served raw. The acid from the fresh lime juice cooks the seafood much more quickly than you'd think.

1 pound (455 g) **halibut fillets** (can substitute snapper fillets), cut into ¼-inch (6 mm) cubes
1 pound (455 g) **large shrimp** (about 15 to 17 per pound), peeled, deveined, rinsed, and roughly chopped
1 cup (240 ml) **fresh lime juice**
⅓ cup (15 g) finely chopped **fresh cilantro**
1½ cups (220 g) chopped **cherry tomatoes**
1 medium **carrot** (2½ ounces/70 g), finely diced
2 **serrano chiles**, stems and seeds removed, finely chopped
½ cup (65 g) finely chopped **red onion**
1 tablespoon **sea salt**

For the habanero crema:
1 to 2 **habanero chiles**, charred (can be grilled directly over the flame on the stovetop)
1 tablespoon **fresh lime juice**
Zest of ½ **lime**
1 teaspoon **sea salt**
Freshly ground black pepper
1 cup (240 ml) **mayonnaise**

For serving:
12 **tostadas** (preferably homemade; recipe on page 52)
1 **avocado**, halved, pitted, peeled, and thinly sliced

In a large bowl, combine the halibut, shrimp, and lime juice and let the seafood marinate for 20 minutes. Drain and discard all but ½ cup (120 ml) of the juice. In the same bowl, add the cilantro, tomatoes, carrot, serranos, red onion, and salt. Stir gently to combine. Refrigerate for an additional 20 minutes.

Meanwhile, make the habanero crema: In a food processor, pulse the charred habanero, lime juice, lime zest, salt, and pepper until finely chopped. Add the mayonnaise and puree until smooth; chill until ready to serve, or up to 30 minutes before serving.

To serve, spread a thin layer of the cilantro mayonnaise on each tostada. Top with the seafood ceviche mixture and garnish with the avocado slices.

Sides

When you invite people to your carne asada, one of the most common responses is: "What can I bring?" Side dishes give your guests the freedom to make a carne asada their own. The way you build your plate says a lot about you: stacking up the meats, loading up on vegetables, or keeping it perfectly balanced and not having anything touching each other. A lot of these dishes aren't grilled. They offer depth and options for when you need a break from the smoke.

PARA

ACOMP AÑAR

Frijoles Puercos con Chorizo y Atún

Serves 6 to 8

These beans taste like home. They are rich and extremely satisfying. We use duck fat instead of the traditional lard for its slightly lighter layer of richness. My mom's original recipe for her frijoles puercos calls for adding canned tuna to the savory bacon and chorizo mix, for yet another layer of umami goodness. I use fresh tuna steaks instead, grilled and chopped over the beans. These beans lend themselves to being spread on a tortilla, tostada, or torta—a little goes a long way.

For the tuna steaks:
¼ teaspoon **dried oregano**
¼ teaspoon **ground coriander**
¼ teaspoon **freshly minced garlic**
½ teaspoon **paprika**
2 tablespoons **soy sauce**
2 tablespoons **grapeseed oil**
12 ounces (340 g) **tuna steaks**, 1 inch (2.5 cm) thick
Sea salt and **freshly ground black pepper**

For the beans:
1 pound (455 g) **dry Mayocoba (Peruano) beans**, cleaned of any pebbles and rinsed (can substitute pinto beans)
1 large **white onion** (10½ ounces/300 g), quartered
1 tablespoon plus ¼ teaspoon **sea salt**, plus more as needed
½ cup (120 ml) **rendered duck fat**
6 **corn tortillas** (preferably homemade; recipes on pages 48 and 51)
2 **cloves garlic**, peeled
3 **dried chiles de árbol**
½ teaspoon **ground cumin**
½ teaspoon **dried oregano**
1 medium **shallot** (2 ounces/55 g), minced
4 ounces (115 g) **bacon**, chopped
12 ounces (340 g) **Mexican chorizo**, removed from casing and crumbled
1 tablespoon **Huichol brand bottled hot sauce**
2 ounces (25 g) **cotija cheese**, grated

Prepare the tuna steaks: In a large bowl, mix together the oregano, coriander, garlic, paprika, soy sauce, and 1 tablespoon of the grapeseed oil. Season the tuna steaks generously with salt and pepper on both sides. Add to the marinade and let rest for 30 minutes.

Meanwhile, prepare the beans: Add the dried beans and the onion to a large pot. Add enough water to cover the beans, about two inches, and bring to a boil. Lower the heat to a simmer, cover, and cook until the beans are softened, about 1 hour. Add 1 tablespoon of the salt to the pot once the beans are cooked. Discard the onion. Turn off heat and let the beans rest rest for 15 minutes.

While the beans are cooking, return to the marinated tuna. Pat it dry using paper towels. Preheat the remaining 1 tablespoon grapeseed oil in a medium cast-iron pan or frying pan over high heat until the oil is almost smoking. Working in batches as needed, cook the tuna in the hot oil for 3 minutes on each side. Remove the tuna from the pan and set aside.

Lower the heat to medium under the same frying pan and add the duck fat. When the fat is hot, gently add the corn tortillas. Let them cook until golden brown, about 1 minute per side. Remove the tortillas and place them on a wide plate or a cooling rack lined with paper towels. Sprinkle with the remaining ¼ teaspoon salt while the tortillas are still warm. Set aside to enjoy with the beans later.

continued

Return the burner to medium heat and fry the garlic and chiles in the duck fat until both are crispy and aromatic, about 5 minutes. Remove from the duck fat and place with the tortillas. Leave the pan with the fat on the burner.

Using a slotted spoon, transfer the cooked beans to a blender with 1 cup (240 ml) of the cooking liquid. Add the fried garlic and chiles, the cumin, and oregano. Pulse three to four times for 1 second each time, just until the bean mixture is chunky, but not all the way pureed. Alternatively, you may use an immersion blender for this, if you have one.

Remove about 2 tablespoons fat from the pan and add the shallot, bacon, and chorizo. Cook until all the ingredients are crispy, about 12 minutes. Slowly and carefully add the blended beans. Cook until they start to simmer and the texture changes. Season with salt to taste. Stir in the hot sauce. Remove from the heat.

Cut the tuna into cubes and layer over the beans. Finish the beans with a sprinkle of grated cotija. Serve with the tortillas.

Frijoles Charros in Broth

Serves 4 to 6

These are your more old-school type of frijoles charros in broth, named after the kind of rustic cooking cowboys would make for themselves while out in the rancho wrangling the cows. They are a classic choice that never fails at a carne asada gathering—or make a big pot for your yourself or your family to enjoy throughout the week.

2 pounds (910 g) **dry pinto beans**, cleaned of any pebbles and rinsed

1 large **white onion** (10½ ounces/300 g), quartered

1 head **garlic** (1¼ ounces/35 g), smashed and peeled

1 tablespoon **sea salt**, plus more as needed

4 ounces (120 g) **bacon** (about 8 strips), chopped

6 ounces (175 g) **deli-sliced ham** (about 8 slices)

6 **hot dogs**, chopped into small pieces

½ teaspoon **ground cumin**

¾ cup (100 g) crumbled **Mexican chorizo**

½ cup (75 g) chopped **Spanish chorizo**

2½ cups (400 g) chopped **tomatoes**

1 cup (40 g) chopped **cilantro**

In a large pot, combine 1 gallon (about 4 L) water with the dried beans, onion, and garlic. Bring to a boil. Once boiling, lower the heat to a simmer, cover, and cook until the beans are softened. This should take about 1 hour but can take up to 2 hours, depending on the freshness of the dried beans. Add the salt to the pot once the beans are cooked. Discard the onion and garlic. Turn off the heat.

In a large frying pan over high heat, add the bacon, ham, hot dogs, ground cumin, and Mexican and Spanish chorizos. Fry until the meat is cooked, about 7 minutes. Add the tomatoes and cook until their liquid is reduced, about 6 minutes. Add this chorizo mixture to the pot of beans and stir to combine. Bring to a simmer and cook for an additional 20 minutes.

Stir in the cilantro. If you would like a thicker broth, mash the contents of the pot with a potato masher. Taste and adjusts seasoning before serving. You can make these beans ahead. If so, wait and stir in the cilantro just before serving.

Frijoles Negros de la Olla con Nopalitos

Serves 6

Nopalitos are much more than an underrated green Mexican vegetable packed with fiber and vitamins; for some of us, those spiky dark green paddles reflect our identity. When cooked, nopales take on a surprisingly meaty texture. Think of these as the vegetarian version of Frijoles Puercos con Chorizo y Atún (page 129).

2 pounds (910 g) **dry black beans**, rinsed and soaked in water for at least 2 hours or overnight
6 **cloves garlic** (⅔ ounce/18 g), peeled and smashed
1 large **white onion** (10½ ounces/300 g), peeled and quartered
3 **cactus paddles (nopalitos)** (10½ ounces/300 g), thorns removed, chopped into 1-inch (2.5 cm) squares
2 tablespoons **sea salt**
2 sprigs **fresh epazote**, rinsed

For serving:
Crumbled **queso fresco**
Tortillas (preferably homemade; recipes on pages 46–51)
Salsa Almendrada (page 210)
Salsa de Chile Ancho en Escabeche (page 187)

How to Deal with Nopales
The greatest señora secret about trimming and dealing with the sharp thorns found on nopales is to burn them off over a flame. To do this, set your range's strongest burner on high and use kitchen tongs to hover individual paddles over the flame. The sharp part of the thorns will burn right off, and they will be much easier to handle. To trim the thorns off the nopales, first slice the edges off. You can do this with a vegetable peeler if the thorns are small, or just carefully slice them off with a paring knife going with the groove of the thorn (not against). The rest of the thorns can be removed easily by slicing them off with a paring knife or peeler.

In a large pot, combine the beans, 2 quarts (2 L) water, the garlic, and onion. Bring to a boil.

Meanwhile, in a bowl, combine the cactus paddles with 1 tablespoon of the salt. Allow to rest until the nopales have softened and released all of their slime, about 20 minutes. Rinse well and set aside.

Once the pot of beans is boiling, lower the heat to a simmer, cover, and cook until the beans are softened. This should take about 1 hour if the beans have been soaked overnight, or half an hour more if they have not. After the beans are tender, discard the onion and garlic. Stir in the cured nopales, epazote, and the remaining tablespoon of salt. Remove from the heat. Allow to rest for 20 minutes, covered.

Serve in bowls with a slice of queso fresco, tortillas, and the salsas.

Frijoles de la Olla

Serves 4

There is a famous Mexican saying that goes: ¡Hay frijoles en la casa! It was the five most-dreaded words you could hear as a kid. It meant you hardly got to go out to eat at restaurants because, more likely than not, there was a pot of perfectly delicious beans at home that would make a complete meal. As a kid, you take the nutritional powerhouse that is a bowl of beans with tortillas for granted. As an adult, you realize that a good pot of beans is actually a lot harder than it looks to make. It's all in the freshness of the beans and of course, patience.

1 pound (455 g) **dry beans**, cleaned of any pebbles and rinsed (We recommend Flor de Mayo, bayos, or pinto beans.)
1 tablespoon **rendered duck fat**
½ large **white onion** (150 g), quartered
1 large sprig **fresh epazote**
2 **cloves garlic**, peeled and smashed
Sea salt
Warm tortillas (preferably homemade; recipes on pages 46–51)

Heat the duck fat in a heavy stockpot over medium heat. Add the onion and cook until translucent, about 5 minutes. Add the epazote, garlic, and the beans. Add enough water to cover by 4 inches (10 cm). Cover and bring to a boil. After the beans have come to a boil, reduce the heat to a simmer and cook until the skins are tender, about 1 hour. Add the salt and continue to cook until the beans are soft but not falling apart. This will take anywhere from 1 to 2 hours, depending on the age and quality of the beans.

If at any time the water level seems too low, add some hot water—never add cold water or the beans will harden and become unappealingly dark.

Serve in bowls with warm tortillas.

Frijoles Refritos

Makes 4 cups (960 g)

Being able to whip up refried beans at a moment's notice almost feels like a superpower. They are great to have at the ready in your refrigerator or freezer. The Oaxacan way of making them is more labor intensive than the usual refried beans found around Mexico, but the flavor that you develop is worth it. Avocado leaves add a deep, anise-like flavor. You can buy them dried online, or find them at some Mexican markets.

3 **chiles de árbol**, stems removed
5 **dried avocado leaves**
4 cups (720 g) **cooked black beans**, drained,
　1 cup (240 ml) bean broth reserved
¼ cup (60 ml) **grapeseed oil**
½ small **white onion** (2 ounces/30 grams), finely
　chopped
Sea salt

In a comal or large cast-iron skillet over medium heat, mix together the chiles and avocado leaves and toast for about 3 minutes. Remove from the heat.

In a blender, blend the beans, reserved bean broth, and the toasted chile–avocado leaf mixture until smooth.

Heat the oil in a large frying pan over medium heat. When hot, stir in the onion and blended bean mixture. Continue stirring as the mixture comes to a boil, scooping and folding the beans into each other over and over again. Be vigilant about not allowing them to stick to the pan. Keep stirring for about 20 minutes total.

Once the refried beans reach a dough-like consistency and they are not runny, they are ready to serve. You can make these beans a day in advance and reheat them with a little water to thin them down.

Arroz Rojo

Serves 8

Many of us grow up eating this Mexican-style red rice with so many dishes. It is a classic side dish that rounds out a carne asada menu. It may look unassuming, but mastering rice takes practice. The more you make it, the more al dente and fluffy you can get it to be. It's all about the ratio of rice to liquid and taking the time to simmer it.

2 cups (390 g) **jasmine rice**
1 (15-ounce/430 g) can **tomatoes in juice**, drained
½ large **white onion** (5¼ ounces/150 g), chopped
2 **cloves garlic**, peeled and halved
1½ tablespoons (20 ml) **grapeseed oil**
1¾ cups (420 ml) **chicken broth**
1 tablespoon **sea salt**
¼ cup (35 g) **frozen peas**
¼ cup (35 g) diced **carrots**
¼ cup (13 g) chopped **fresh flat-leaf parsley**
2 fresh **serrano chiles**

Place the rice in a mixing bowl and cover with cool water. Swirl the rice in the water, mixing it around with your hands. Pour off the water and repeat three more times, or until the water is clear. Drain the rice.

In a blender, puree the tomatoes, onion, and garlic. Set aside.

In a large sauté pan with a tight-fitting lid, heat the oil over medium heat. When hot, add the rice and cook, stirring regularly, until the grains become translucent. This takes about 4 to 5 minutes.

Stir in the pureed tomato mixture. Cook until the liquid is reduced and the mixture is somewhat dry, looking about 2 to 3 minutes. Add the broth, salt, peas, carrots, and parsley and stir thoroughly. Top with the chiles, cover, and cook over the lowest heat setting for 15 minutes.

Remove the rice from the heat and let stand with the cover on for about 5 minutes. Fluff the rice with a fork. Cover and let rest for 15 minutes.

Uncover and allow the rice to cool for 15 more minutes. This will allow it to achieve the perfect fluff.

Arroz Verde

Serves 4

This green rice gets its stunning color from fresh green chiles and cilantro. It is perhaps the tastiest way to eat more green foods, and more likely than not will have people asking you for the recipe.

1 cup (185 g) **jasmine rice**
2 **fresh poblano chiles**, stems and seeds removed, cut in half
1 ear **corn**, husk on
½ medium **white onion** (3½ ounces/100 g), quartered
4 **cloves garlic**, peeled
1 cup (40 g) chopped **fresh cilantro**
1 tablespoon **apple cider vinegar**
2 tablespoons **grapeseed oil**
¾ cup + 2 tablespoons (210 ml) chicken broth
1½ teaspoons sea salt
1 serrano chile

Place the rice in a mixing bowl and cover with cool water. Swirl the rice in the water and mix around with your hands. Pour off the water and repeat three times or until the water is clear. Drain the rice.

Start a charcoal or gas grill. The gas should be set to high. If using a pellet grill, preheat your grill to 425°F (220°C) for at least 15 minutes. If using charcoal, the coals should be red but entirely covered with gray ash.

Place the poblanos, corn, and onion directly on the grill. Grill for about 8 minutes, flipping once, until charred. Remove to a plate.

Shuck the ear of corn and shave off the kernels. Set aside. In a blender or food processor, puree the charred poblanos, onion, and garlic with the cilantro, ¼ cup (60 ml) water, and the vinegar until smooth.

In a large sauté pan with a tight-fitting lid, heat the oil over medium heat. When hot, add the rice, corn kernels. Cook, stirring regularly until the rice grains become translucent. This takes about 4 to 5 minutes.

Stir the pureed poblano mixture into the vegetable mixture. Cook until the liquid is semi-reduced, about 1 to 2 minutes.

Pour in the broth and stir thoroughly. Bring to a boil. Top with chile, cover, and cook over the lowest heat setting for 15 minutes. Remove from the heat and let stand for about 5 minutes. Fluff the rice with a fork and turn off the heat. Cover and let rest for 15 more minutes.

Uncover and allow to cool for about 15 minutes. This will allow the rice to achieve the perfect fluff.

Arroz Blanco

Serves 4

Sometimes, all you are craving is some simple fluffy white rice. Not seasoned with tomatoes or with fresh chiles. Using chicken stock to cook your rice adds so much savory flavor and makes it taste buttery. This rice is the definition of comfort food.

1 cup (185 g) **jasmine rice**
2 cups (480 ml) **chicken broth**
2 **cloves garlic**, peeled
½ large **white onion** (5¼ ounces/150 g), peeled and quartered
2 small **tomatillos**, husked and rinsed
2 tablespoons **grapeseed oil**
Sea salt
1 sprig **parsley**

Place the rice in a mixing bowl and cover with cool water. Swirl the rice in the water and mix around with your hands. Pour off the water and repeat three times or until the water is clear. Drain the rice.

In a blender, combine the chicken broth with the garlic, onion, and tomatillos. Blend until smooth, then pass through a double fine-mesh strainer. Reserve.

In a large sauté pan with a tight-fitting lid, heat the oil over medium heat. When hot, add the rice. Cook, stirring regularly, until the rice grains become translucent. This takes about 4 to 5 minutes.

Add the pureed mixture. Stir. Add salt to taste and the sprig of parsley as a garnish on top of the rice and bring to a boil. Lower the heat to a simmer, cover, and let cook for 15 minutes or until the rice is tender.

Uncover and allow to cool for about 15 minutes. This will allow the rice to achieve the perfect fluff.

Elotes Asados with Roasted Garlic Butter

Serves 4 to 8

Slathering some grilled corn with butter, mayonnaise, cotija cheese, lime, and chile powder is as Mexican as the Mexican national anthem. It has become an iconic street food, and you'll see it around the world on menus at Mexican and non-Mexican restaurants alike. I like to add some roasted garlic to our elotes to make it even more savory. Half the fun is getting it all over your face! There is just something uniquely satisfying about picking off every last kernel on a cob with your teeth. The only other sensation that comes close is eating meat off a bone. I leave some corn on the grill a little longer until some kernels are charred extra well-done for those who prefer it *bien quemadito* (well-charred!). You know who you are . . .

1 head **garlic**, peels on, cut in half crosswise
1 tablespoon **unsalted butter**
4 ears **corn**, husks on
1 cup (240 ml) **mayonnaise**
1 teaspoon **ground coriander**
½ teaspoon **sea salt**
1 tablespoon **fresh lime juice**
½ cup (60 g) **crumbled cotija**
2 tablespoons **piquin chile powder** or **ancho chile powder**

Start a charcoal or gas grill. The gas should be set to high. If using a pellet grill, preheat your grill to 425°F (220°C) for at least 15 minutes. If using charcoal, the coals should be red but entirely covered with gray ash.

Lay the garlic on a square sheet of aluminum foil, brush with the butter, and wrap tightly.

Place the corn and wrapped garlic directly on the grill. Grill the garlic for about 40 minutes, undisturbed. Grill the corn for about 45 minutes, flipping once. Remove both from the grill.

In a bowl, mix the mayonnaise, coriander, salt, and lime juice. Add the pulp of the roasted garlic by squeezing the head like you would squeeze a lime. Stir to combine.

Pull back the husks from the top down. Spread the garlic mayonnaise all over each ear with a brush and sprinkle the cotija cheese all over the mayonnaise. Finish with a sprinkle of ground chile all around. Serve whole, or cut each corn on the cob into thirds.

Esquites

Serves 6

Whole Mexican-style street elote (on the cob; see page 147) versus esquites (shaved corn served in a cup) is one of the greatest food debates. The reality is that there is a place and time for each! When you don't feel like making out with elote on a stick, then it's time for an esquisite, basically an elote *off* the cob, which is a lot easier to eat since practially all the work has been done for you! The corn is neatly packed in a cup. An esquisite also comes with one added bonus that an elote asado cannot offer: a sweet corn broth.

3 tablespoons **grapeseed oil**
½ large **white onion** (5¼ ounces/150 g), finely chopped
1 **serrano chile**
2 **Fresno chiles**, thinly sliced, stems removed
3 cups (290 g) freshly shaved **white corn kernels** (shaved with a chef's knife)
1½ tablespoons **sea salt**, plus more as needed
3 large sprigs **epazote**
½ cup (120 ml) **mayonnaise**
½ teaspoon **ground coriander**
1 tablespoon **red chile powder**
1 cup (150 g) crumbled **queso fresco**

For the garnish:
Key lime slices

In a large pot, heat the oil over medium heat. Add the onion and chiles as is. Cook until the onion is translucent, about 5 minutes. Add the corn kernels and salt. Stir for about 3 minutes, then add 3 cups (720 ml) water and the epazote. Bring to a boil over high heat, reduce the heat to a simmer, and cook, uncovered, until the corn is tender, about 20 minutes. Taste and season with more salt as needed.

Meanwhile, in a small bowl, mix together the mayonnaise and the coriander.

To serve, divide the warm esquites among 6 cups. Top each serving with about 1 tablespoon of the coriander mayo, a sprinkle of the chile powder, and 2½ tablespoons of the crumbled queso fresco. Finish with a squeeze of fresh lime juice.

Grilled Veggies with Pipián Dip

Serves 6 to 8

Vegetarians should never feel unwelcome at a carne asada; they are always welcome at mine. I usually offer at least a few veggie-forward options for them, and anyone else who loves vegetables. If I turn my grill on, I usually like to throw any vegetables I have in the fridge on the grill because there is just something about grilling veggies that makes them taste better than any other way of cooking them.

For the dip:

1 **habanero**, stem removed

4 **cloves garlic**, peeled

3 **red bell peppers** (5¼ ounces/300 g each), stems and seeds removed

2 large **heirloom tomatoes** or **tomatoes on the vine** (14 ounces/400 g)

1 slice **sourdough bread**

½ cup (120 ml) **grapeseed oil**

½ cup (120 ml) **olive oil**

1 cup (140 g) **raw almonds**, lightly toasted in a skillet on the stovetop

¼ cup (60 ml) **red wine vinegar**

2 teaspoons **sea salt**

For the vegetables:

8 ounces (225 g) **heirloom carrots**, trimmed and peeled

½ **yellow squash**, woody nub cut off

8 ounces (225 g) **asparagus**, woody nubs snapped off

8 ounces (225 g) **calabacita** (Mexican summer squash; can substitute zucchini), quartered

¼ cup (60 ml) **olive oil**

1 tablespoon **sea salt**

1 tablespoon **freshly ground black pepper**

Start a charcoal or gas grill. The gas should be set to high. If using a pellet grill, preheat your grill to 425°F (220°C) for at least 15 minutes. If using charcoal, the coals should be red but entirely covered with gray ash.

Make the dip: Wrap the habanero and garlic in a square sheet of aluminum foil. Place the bell peppers, tomatoes, and bread directly on the grill along with the wrapped habanero and garlic. Grill the bread just until charred, about a minute or two per side. Grill the bell pepper and tomatoes for about 10 minutes, flipping constantly until charred. The habanero and garlic will be softened after about 10 minutes. Remove from the grill, and set aside.

In a food processor, blend the habanero, garlic, bell pepper, tomatoes, bread, the grapeseed and olive oils, almonds, vinegar, and salt until the texture is like a paste.

Prepare the vegetables: In a large bowl, toss the carrots, yellow squash, asparagus, and calabacita with the olive oil, salt, and pepper.

Place the vegetables directly on the grill and grill them for about 10 minutes, flipping constantly until they are charred.

Serve the veggies warm with the dip on the side.

Nopales Asados

Serves 4

Nopales asados and carne asada were made for each other. When grilled, these fleshy tender paddles of the nopal cactus absorb all the smoke flavor and are almost impossible to overcook because they are so sturdy and full of moisture. Not to mention that grilling while constantly flipping the nopal paddles at high heat, practically eliminates their naturally occurring slime, which can be off-putting to some.

8 **cactus paddles** (**nopales**) (1¾ pounds/800 g); purchase ones with thorns already removed
2 tablespoons **grapeseed oil**
1 teaspoon **sea salt**

Start a charcoal or gas grill. If using gas, set it to high. If using a pellet grill, preheat your grill to 450°F (230°C) for at least 15 minutes. If using charcoal, the coals should be red but entirely covered with gray ash.

When the grill is preheated, place each nopal on the hot grill, brush them liberally with oil on both sides, and season with salt. Cover and let cook for 10 minutes. After 10 minutes, open the grill and flip them to the other side. Let cook for another 10 minutes. The nopal should turn a toasty brown-green color when cooked.

To serve, slice the nopales into 1-inch (2.5 cm) strips.

Ensalada de Nopalitos

Serves 4

A carne asada is a very salad-friendly affair. All the piles of grilled meat beg for some crisp vegetables to eat them with. If you are only going to offer one salad, this is the one to make. Instead of boiling or grilling nopales, they are cured in salt, which maintains the limelike tartness that these cacti offer and their vibrant green color as well.

8 **cactus paddles (nopalitos)** (1¾ pounds/800 g); purchase ones with thorns already removed
2 tablespoons plus 1 teaspoon **sea salt**
1 tablespoon **olive oil**
1 **clove garlic**, minced
1 **guajillo chile**, stems and seeds removed, cut into thin rings
1 **chile de arbol**, stems and seeds removed
1½ teaspoons **dried Mexican oregano**
1 dash **ground cumin**
Freshly ground black pepper
1 teaspoon **pineapple vinegar** (can substitute citrus vinegar)

Slice the nopales into ½-inch (12 mm) squares; you should have about 4 cups (800 g). In a bowl, toss the nopales with 2 tablespoons of the salt. Allow them to rest until the nopales have softened and released all their slime, about 30 minutes. Rinse well under cold water.

Heat the olive oil in a large pan over medium heat. When hot, add the garlic, chiles, 2 cups (275 g) of the cured nopales, the oregano, cumin, pepper, and remaining 1 teaspoon salt. Cook and stir well for 5 minutes. Add the vinegar, stir for 1 more minute, and remove from the heat.

Toss in the remaining 2 cups (275 g) cured nopales and serve in a large bowl.

Grilled Cebollitas

Serves 4

A carne asada is not complete without tender, charred, spring green onions. The high heat from a grill transforms their inner layers into a sweet and tender texture, while the outside layer gets deliciously charred and the greens a little crispy. When done correctly, you will look forward to the grilled cebollitas at a carne asada as much as the meat itself. Always make more than you think you'll need because they are usually the first to go.

8 **spring onions** (2 to 3 bunches)
2 tablespoons **grapeseed oil**
1 teaspoon **sea salt**
2 tablespoons **fresh lime juice**

Start a charcoal or gas grill. If using gas, set it to high heat. If using a pellet grill, preheat your grill to 450°F (230°C) for at least 15 minutes. If using charcoal, the coals should be red but entirely covered with gray ash.

In a large bowl, mix the onions, stems and all, with the oil and salt.

Place the onions on the grill and cover. Let cook for 20 to 30 minutes, or until the onions are cooked all the way through and the outside is charred and crispy. Alternatively, you can set the onions on the edges of the grill to slowly cook while you grill your meat in the middle of the grill, where it's hotter.

When the onions are done, remove them from the grill and chop them into large pieces to make them easier to eat with your taco. Put them in a bowl and mix thoroughly with the lime juice.

Enjoy over your carne asada taco instead of regular onion, or as a side.

Pickled Red Onions

Makes two 16-ounce (480 ml) jars

Pickled red onions used to be reserved exclusively for cochinita pibil (page 93), but in Los Angeles people started offering them to top everything from birria (a traditional stew made from braised beef or goat) to cabeza (steamed beef or pork head tacos, which is popular across Mexico). With their lightly sweet and refreshingly spicy bite, it's easy to see why. I like to always have some ready to eat because you never know when you're going to crave them.

2 cups (250 g) thinly sliced **red onion** (from about 2 medium onions)
1½ cups (360 ml) **apple cider vinegar**
½ cup (120 ml) **orange juice**, freshly squeezed if in season
⅓ cup (65 g) **sugar**
2 **cloves garlic**, peeled
1 teaspoon **black peppercorns**
2 tablespoons **sea salt**

Divide your sliced onions between two 16-ounce (480 ml) jars.

In a medium saucepan over medium heat, add the vinegar, orange juice, 2 cups (480 ml) water, the sugar, garlic, peppercorns, and salt. Stir until the sugar and salt dissolve, about 1 to 2 minutes. Remove the saucepan from the heat and allow it to cool slightly for 20 minutes.

Pour the warm brine over the onions. Set the jars aside to cool all the way to room temperature, then screw on the lids and store them in the refrigerator.

The pickled onions will be ready to eat once they're bright pink and tender, about 1 hour for very thinly sliced onions, or overnight for thickly sliced onions. Store in your refrigerator for up to 1 month.

Roasted Camotitos

Serves 6

Camotes are an old-school Mexican favorite. In some ranchos in Mexico, they are slowly cooked in a piloncillo syrup (a syrup made from unrefined brown sugar; a traditional ingredient) and served in a bowl, to be mashed with cold milk. In major cities, they are a popular street food sold from a pushcart-turned-portable oven that you can hear a mile away because of a horn that vendors use that sounds like a train whistle. They sound it to let sweet potato-lovers that they are around and ready to serve. In this recipe, we make them extra savory by pairing them with a cumin compound butter.

6 medium **orange-fleshed sweet potatoes** (about 1½ pounds/630 g), scrubbed
2 tablespoons **extra-virgin olive oil**
Sea salt and **freshly ground black pepper**

For the toasted cumin seed compound butter:
1 tablespoon **cumin seeds**, roughly ground
2 tablespoons **pepitas** (pumpkin seeds)
1 tablespoon **sesame seeds**
¼ cup (½ stick; 59 ml) **salted butter**
¼ cup (10 g) chopped **fresh cilantro**
Finishing salt

Preheat your grill to 375°F (190°C) if using a pellet grill, to low heat if using gas, or for indirect cooking if using charcoal, with the lid closed, for 15 minutes.

Prick the sweet potatoes all over with a fork and rub them all over with the olive oil. Season generously with salt and pepper. Grill the sweet potatoes over indirect heat, covered, turning occasionally, until very soft inside, about 45 minutes. For extra char, you can move them to direct heat for the final 10 minutes of cooking.

Make the toasted cumin butter: In a small nonstick pan over medium heat, toast the semi-crushed cumin seeds, the pepitas, and sesame seeds until fragrant, about 5 minutes. Add the butter to the pan and let it melt, shaking the pan occasionally. Stir in the cilantro and remove the pan from the heat.

To serve, cut a slit down the center of each sweet potato and top with spoonfuls of the cumin seed butter and lots of flaky salt. Serve immediately.

Grilled Romaine Ensalada Caesar con Miso

Serves 6

One of my favorite fun facts to drop on unsuspecting people is that Caesar salad is Mexican food. The hotel it was created in, Caesar's Hotel in Tijuana, is still up and running, and cranking out Caesar salads by the dozens every day, freshly made tableside. Going to Tijuana to have it with a glass of Mexican wine made in Valle de Guadalupe nearby is definitely something to experience at least once. I love the original with anchovies, but one time I had it with miso while wine tasting in Napa, and I've been making it with this ever since.

For the croutons:
3 thick slices **country bread**, cut into 1-inch (2.5 cm) cubes
½ cup (120 ml) **extra-virgin olive oil**
Sea salt and **freshly ground black pepper**

For the dressing:
2 **cloves garlic**, mashed into a paste
2 tablespoons **Dijon mustard**
2 tablespoons **mellow white miso**
2 large **egg yolks**
¼ cup (120 ml) **fresh lime juice**
1 teaspoon **Worcestershire sauce**
¼ teaspoon **freshly ground black pepper**, plus more to taste
1 cup (240 ml) **extra-virgin olive oil**
½ cup (60 g) grated **cotija cheese**
Sea salt

For the salad and garnishes:
2 large heads **romaine lettuce**
Extra-virgin olive oil, for drizzling
Grated **cotija cheese**, for serving
Freshly ground black pepper, for serving

Make the croutons: Preheat the oven to 400°F (200°C).

In a large bowl, toss together the bread cubes and olive oil. Add salt and pepper to taste and toss again. Transfer the bread cubes to a baking sheet, spreading them out in an even layer. Bake for 8 to 10 minutes, toss, and return to the oven for another 8 minutes, or until golden and crispy. Set the pan aside and let the croutons cool to room temperature.

Make the dressing: In a medium bowl, use a fork to mash together the garlic paste, Dijon, and miso until smooth. Add the egg yolks and whisk vigorously until the yolks are fully incorporated and uniform. Add the lime juice, Worcestershire sauce, and pepper and whisk again to combine. Very slowly stream in the olive oil, whisking continuously, until fully emulsified into the dressing. Stir in the cotija and taste for seasoning. (You may not need any salt at all due to the miso, but feel free to add if needed.) Cover and chill the dressing until ready to serve.

Make the salad: Start a charcoal or gas grill. The gas should be set to medium. If using a pellet grill, preheat your grill to 350°F (175°C) for at least 15 minutes. If using charcoal, the coals should be red but entirely covered with gray ash.

continued

Remove any wilted or browning outer leaves from the lettuce. Trim off just a little of the root ends (too much and the heads will fall apart) and cut the lettuce heads in half lengthwise. Drizzle the lettuce halves generously with olive oil.

Grill the lettuce, cut side down, for 5 minutes over direct heat, until nicely charred.

To serve family style, cut the grilled lettuce halves crosswise into 4-inch (10 cm) sections and arrange them on a serving platter. Top generously with the dressing and then scatter the croutons over the top. Sprinkle cotija over everything, followed by several cracks of pepper, and serve immediately.

Tossed Elotes

Serves 6

This genius salad transforms a roasted poblano chile into a dressing. It uses a lot of the staple ingredients found in a Mexican family's kitchen, but in a slightly different way. When it's peak corn season and fresh corn is tasting its sweetest, this salad feels like the best side dish for a carne asada of all time.

5 ears sweet **white corn**, shucked and halved crosswise
1 **poblano chile** (3½ ounces/100 g), cored, stems and seeds removed, cut in half
⅓ cup (75 ml) **fresh lemon juice**
½ cup (120 ml) **olive oil**
2 tablespoons **champagne vinegar**
1 teaspoon **cane sugar**
½ teaspoon **ground cumin**
¼ teaspoon **finely minced garlic**
1 tablespoon plus 1 teaspoon **whole-grain mustard**
2 teaspoons **sea salt**
1 teaspoon **cayenne pepper**

For the garnishes:
½ cup (15 g) roughly chopped **fresh parsley**
½ cup (60 g) crumbled **fresh cotija**

Start a charcoal or gas grill. The gas should be set to high. If using a pellet grill, preheat your grill to 425°F (220°C) for at least 15 minutes. If using charcoal, the coals should be red but entirely covered with gray ash.

Place the corn and poblano directly on the grill. Grill them for about 20 minutes, flipping constantly, until charred. Remove from the grill. In a blender, add the roasted poblano, lemon juice, olive oil, vinegar, sugar, cumin, garlic, mustard, salt, and cayenne. Blend until smooth.

Remove the corn kernels by standing the cob upright and carefully shaving the kernels off from top to bottom using a chef's knife. Rotate the cob to make sure to shave all sides of the corn.

Toss the corn with the poblano dressing. Top the salad with the chopped parsley and fresh cotija.

This tossed elote can be made up to 5 hours ahead.

Cucumber and Radish Taquero Salad

Serves 4

We call this a taquero salad because you can make it easily with the ingredients found at a taquería. Besides the fiber, vitamins, and all that good stuff, radishes and cucumber provide a much-needed fresh contrast to your carne asada. And occasionally the only vegetables that you will eat in a day are the slices of spicy radish and cucumber that are served with your tacos. That's just how life goes sometimes.

¼ cup (60 ml) **fresh lime juice**
2 tablespoons **olive oil**
1 tablespoon **sea salt**
2 teaspoons **freshly ground black pepper**
8 **radishes** (about 2 bunches), greens removed and edges trimmed, thinly sliced on a mandoline
2 **Persian cucumbers**, thinly sliced (You can use a mandoline as well.)
¼ cup (13 g) minced **fresh mint**

In a large bowl, whisk the lime juice and olive oil until emulsified. Add the salt and pepper and whisk to combine.

Add the radishes, cucumbers, and mint to the bowl. Mix around so that the dressing evenly coats the vegetables. Let sit for at least 30 minutes before serving so the vegetables can absorb the flavors of the dressing.

Epazote-Roasted Mushroom Queso Fundido

Serves 6

A pro move is to spoon some of this queso on your tortilla and then layer some carne asada over that for a makeshift mulita. This one is also vegetarian friendly. Don't be afraid to dive in and expect some of the best cheese-pulls of your life.

¼ cup (60 ml) **fresh lime juice**
¼ cup (60 ml) **extra-virgin olive oil**
4 tablespoons (13 g) chopped **fresh epazote**
1 teaspoon **apple cider vinegar**
1 **clove garlic**, grated
Sea salt and **freshly ground black pepper**
Pinch **red chile flakes**
6 ounces (170 g) **mixed mushrooms**, such as cremini, button, or white or brown birch, quartered
1 pound (455 g) **queso Oaxaca**, shredded
Fresh tortillas or **tortilla chips**, for serving

Preheat the oven to 350°F (175°C).

In a medium bowl, whisk together the lime juice, olive oil, 3 tablespoons of the epazote, the vinegar, and garlic and season with salt, pepper, and chile flakes. Add the mushrooms and toss to coat. Set aside to marinate at room temperature for 30 minutes.

In a medium cast-iron pan, add the shredded Oaxaca cheese and the remaining tablespoon epazote. Stir to combine and put the pan in the oven for about 20 minutes, until the cheese is fully melted.

While the cheese is melting, add the mushrooms and their marinade to another cast-iron or nonstick pan and cook over medium-high heat, stirring occasionally, until the mushrooms are deeply bronzed and nearly crispy on the edges, 15 to 20 minutes.

Gently spoon the mushroom mixture in the center of the melted cheese. Serve the queso immediately in the pan with the tortillas or tortilla chips.

Choriqueso Fundido

Serves 6

The cheese pulls that this choriqueso fundido creates are legendary; it was made for entertaining. On its own, with some great salsa, it can be a quick and extremely satisfying meal.

4 ounces (113 g) **Mexican chorizo**, in casing
10 ounces (280 g) **queso Oaxaca**, cut into cubes
1 tablespoon chopped **fresh parsley**
1 tablespoon minced **fresh basil**

Start a charcoal or gas grill. The gas should be set to high. If using a pellet grill, preheat your grill to 425°F (220°C) for at least 15 minutes. If using charcoal, the coals should be red but entirely covered with gray ash.

Place the chorizo directly on the grill. Grill the chorizo for about 10 minutes, flipping twice, until charred and cooked through. Remove from the grill and set aside to cool.

Once the chorizo is cool enough to handle, remove from the casing and crumble the sausage.

Place a small cast-iron skillet directly on the grill and add the cubed queso Oaxaca. Close the lid and allow the cheese to melt, undisturbed, for about 3 to 5 minutes. Top with the crumbled chorizo in the middle of the melted cheese and sprinkle with the parsley and basil. Serve warm.

Zucchinis con Queso y Salsa Roja

Serves 4 to 6

If you're looking for a vegetarian main course to offer at a carne asada, these stuffed zucchini lend themselves to being grilled and take on a great smoky flavor.

For the zucchini:
4 medium **zucchinis**
1 tablespoon **olive oil**
1 **clove garlic**, minced
1½ tablespoons diced **white onion**
¼ cup (30 g) **panko bread crumbs**
1 large **egg**
Sea salt, plus more for the cooking water
5 ounces (140 g) **queso Oaxaca**, grated
2 tablespoons minced **fresh parsley**
2 tablespoons minced **fresh basil**

For the salsa:
3 medium **roma tomatoes** (200 g)
1 **clove garlic**, peeled
2 tablespoons (75 g) minced **white onion**
1 tablespoon **olive oil**
1 teaspoon **sea salt**
Freshly ground black pepper

Prepare the zucchini: Slice the zucchini in half lengthwise and use a spoon to scoop out the seeded flesh. Roughly chop the flesh. Set the hollowed-out zucchini halves aside.

Heat the olive oil in a large frying pan over medium heat. Once hot, add the garlic and onion and cook for 2 to 3 minutes. Add the chopped zucchini flesh and cook for 2 to 3 more minutes. Remove the zucchini mixture from the heat. Add the bread crumbs and the egg and mix thoroughly to combine.

Bring a large pot of salted water to a boil, add the hollowed-out zucchini halves, and briefly cook until they soften slightly, about 3 minutes. Remove the zucchini from the boiling water to a plate and sprinkle them with salt. Stuff a couple of tablespoons of the seasoned flesh into the zucchini halves and top with the grated cheese.

Make the salsa: Preheat your grill to 375°F (190°C) if using a pellet grill, to low heat if using gas, or for indirect cooking if using charcoal, with the lid closed, for 15 minutes.

Place the tomatoes directly on the grill. Wrap the garlic and onion in aluminum foil and add the package to the grill. Cover the grill and let the tomatoes char for 15 minutes. Once charred, put the tomatoes, onion, and garlic in a blender and add the olive oil, salt, and pepper. Blend until the salsa is chunky and the ingredients are evenly mixed. Reserve for later.

Place the stuffed zucchinis directly on the grill. Close the lid and allow the cheese to melt, undisturbed, for about 15 minutes.

Sprinkle the stuffed zucchini with the parsley and basil and serve with the sauce.

Queso and Squash Flower Poblanos

Serves 4

In Mexico, usually, squash blossoms are tucked into a quesadilla. Since they are so delicate, they become tender with just the heat of the melted cheese. Here, we give them the carne asada treatment and stuff them in a chile to grill them.

4 **poblano chiles** (14 ounces/400 g)
Sea salt
8 ounces (225 g) **queso Oaxaca**, shredded
8 **squash blossoms**
4 sprigs **epazote**
1 tablespoon minced **fresh parsley**
1 tablespoon minced **fresh mint**

Start a charcoal or gas grill. The gas should be set to high. If using a pellet grill, preheat your grill to 425°F (220°C) for at least 15 minutes. If using charcoal, the coals should be red but entirely covered with gray ash.

Place the poblanos directly on the grill. Cook until the skin is completely charred and the flesh is somewhat soft, about 10 minutes. Turn the poblanos every 2 to 3 minutes for even cooking.

Once the chiles are charred, put them in a medium bowl and cover with a large plate for a few minutes to soften and steam. This will make peeling the burnt skin off easier. When cool enough to handle, remove most of the skin with your fingers.

Cut a small slit in each poblano, about 2 inches (5 cm) long, starting at the stem end. Remove the seeds carefully, so as not to break the chiles. Sprinkle with salt. Stuff each chile with the cheese, squash blossoms, and epazote, dividing the ingredients evenly.

Put the chiles directly over the grill again. Close the lid and allow the cheese to melt, undisturbed, for about 5 minutes. Serve warm.

Taco Encuerado

Serves 6

This taco gets its provocative name because it is just a simple grilled chile, stuffed with cheese—"naked" on a charred tortilla. That's it. No salsa is necessary, just a sprinkling of salt.

6 fresh **Hatch chiles** (1⅓ pounds/600 g; can substitute fresh Anaheim chiles)
10 ounces (280 g) **queso Oaxaca**
12 fresh **epazote leaves**
6 **warm flour tortillas** (preferably homemade; recipe on page 46)
Finishing salt

Start a charcoal or gas grill. The gas should be set to medium. If using a pellet grill, preheat your grill to 375°F (190°C) for at least 15 minutes. If using charcoal, the coals should be red but entirely covered with gray ash.

Place the chiles directly on the grill. Cook until the skin is completely charred and the flesh is somewhat soft, about 5 to 7 minutes. Turn the chiles every 2 to 3 minutes for even cooking.

Once the chiles are charred, put them in a medium bowl and cover with a large plate for a few minutes to soften and steam. This will make peeling the burnt skin off easier. When cool enough to handle, remove most of the skin with your fingers.

Cut a small slit in each chile, about 3 inches (7.5 cm) long, starting at the stem end. Remove the seeds carefully, so as not to break the chiles. Stuff each chile with the cheese and epazote, dividing the ingredients evenly.

Put the chiles directly on the grill again. Close the lid and allow the cheese to melt, undisturbed, for about 3 to 5 minutes.

Serve on top of warm flour tortillas. Sprinkle with finishing salt.

A salsa makes a taco. People will always remember your salsa at a carne asada. A good salsa is a thrill! It gets your endorphins going and keeps you taking more and more bites. It ties all the meats, side dishes, and vegetables together. Most of these salsas can be made a day ahead. Just make sure to bring back to room temperature before serving.

LAS SALSAS

Chile De
Arbol Tostado
$ 6.99 Lb.

Salsa Verde

Makes 2 cups (480 ml)

Learning how to make a great salsa verde is as valuable as learning how to scramble some eggs for breakfast. One of the most versatile salsas you can make, it tastes great on everything from beef to chicken to pork.

8½ ounces (250 g) **green tomatillos milperos**, husked and washed

4 **serrano chiles** (3¼ ounces/90 g)

½ large **white onion** (5¼ ounces/150 g), quartered

2 **cloves garlic**, peeled

1 teaspoon **dried Mexican oregano**

½ teaspoon **cane sugar**

1 cup (40 g) loosely packed **fresh cilantro**, leaves and tender stems only

½ teaspoon **ground coriander**

2 tablespoons **grapeseed oil**

1 teaspoon **sea salt**

In a saucepan over medium heat, add the tomatillos, serranos, onion, garlic, oregano, cane sugar, and ¼ cup (60 ml) water. Stir and cook until the tomatillos have softened, about 10 minutes.

In a blender or food processor, blend the tomatillo mixture with the cilantro and ground coriander until smooth. Set aside.

In a medium saucepan, heat the oil over medium heat. Add the salsa and bring to a boil. Remove from the heat, season with the salt, and allow to cool before serving.

186

Salsa de Chile Ancho en Escabeche

Makes 2 cups (480 ml)

If you love salsa macha (Mexico's famous nut-and-oil-based salsa), you will love this oil-and-vinegar-based salsa. It is great on cheese in a quesadilla or seafood.

14 **ancho chiles** (8½ ounces/250 g), stems and seeds removed
½ cup (60 ml) **grapeseed oil**
1 cup (125 g) finely sliced **white onion**
1 large head **garlic** (12 cloves), peeled
2 cups (480 ml) **pineapple vinegar** (can substitute apple cider vinegar)
¼ cup (35 g) grated **piloncillo**
10 **black peppercorns**
5 **whole allspice berries**
3 sprigs **marjoram**
3 sprigs **thyme**
3 **bay leaves**
1 teaspoon **sea salt**

Cut each chile into 4 long strips.

Heat the oil in a wide pan over medium-low heat. Add the chile strips, one by one, pressing them down with a flat spatula, until they change color, about 30 to 45 seconds each. Be careful not to burn them. Remove the chiles from the pan and set them aside on a plate lined with paper towels.

In the same pan, cook the onion and garlic until the onion is translucent and the garlic has softened, about 5 minutes. Remove from the heat and set aside.

In another saucepan over medium heat, add the vinegar, piloncillo, peppercorns, allspice, marjoram, thyme, bay leaves, and salt. Allow the mixture to come to a boil, then remove from the heat.

In a large jar with a lid, add the chiles, onion, and garlic, alternating between each one. Cover with the vinegar mixture.

Allow to cool at room temperature, then store in the refrigerator for at least 2 hours or up to 3 days before serving.

Salsa Asada de Aguacate

Makes 2 cups (480 ml)

There can never be enough uses for avocado. It can find its way into recipes in many forms, and this salsa, somewhere between a salsa verde and a taquería-style guacamole, is one of my favorites.

14 ounces (400 g) **tomatillos**, preferably the milapero variety, husked and rinsed
4 **serrano chiles** (3 ounces/90 g), stems removed
1 **spring onion** or 2 **green onions**
1 **clove garlic**, peeled
2 cups (80 g) loosely packed **fresh cilantro**, leaves and tender stems only
1 teaspoon **sea salt**
2 small **avocados**, pitted and peeled

Start a charcoal or gas grill. Gas should be set to high. If using a pellet grill, preheat your grill to 425°F (220°C) for at least 15 minutes. If using charcoal, the coals should be red but entirely covered with gray ash.

Cook the tomatillos, serranos, and onion directly on the grill until their skins have charred evenly, about 7 to 15 minutes. Turn every 3 to 4 minutes for even cooking. Remove to a plate.

In a food processor, add the tomatillos, serranos, onion, garlic, cilantro, and salt. Pulse until a smooth paste forms, adding up to 2 tablespoons water to loosen the salsa as needed. Add the avocados and pulse again. Serve within 1 hour.

Salsa Verde con Aguacate

Makes 2 cups (480 ml)

If you are the type of person who prefers to add a slice of avocado to tacos instead of guacamole, this salsa is a nice compromise. It maintains the integrity of the buttery avocado since it is cubed and added in the end.

2 **cloves garlic**, peeled

1 pound (450 g) **tomatillos**, preferably the milpero variety, husked and rinsed

2 **serrano chiles**

2 **jalapeños**

1 teaspoon **salt**

1 cup (40 g) chopped **fresh cilantro**

1 large **avocado**, pitted, cubed, and peeled

Start a charcoal or gas grill. Gas should be set to high. If using a pellet grill, preheat your grill to 425°F (220°C) for at least 15 minutes. If using charcoal, the coals should be red but entirely covered with gray ash.

Wrap the garlic in aluminum foil and place the wrapped garlic, tomatillos, serranos, and jalapeños directly on the grill. Cook until the skins of the tomatillos and chiles have charred evenly, about 7 to 15 minutes. Turn every 3 to 4 minutes for even cooking. The garlic should be softened and charred in about 10 minutes. Remove to a plate.

In a food processor, add the garlic, tomatillos, chiles, and salt with ¼ cup (60 ml) water. Pulse until smooth. Pour the sauce into a bowl and gently mix in the cilantro and avocado. Serve immediately, or refrigerate for up to 6 hours.

191

Salsa Taquera en Molcajete

Makes 2 cups (480 ml)

There is something about making a salsa in a molcajete that makes it taste better. I swear that something magical happens when you crush chiles between two pieces of stone that no blender will ever replicate. We like to bust out the molcajete to make a salsa as regularly as we can to remind us of this magic and continue this ancient tradition with my children.

17½ ounces (500 g) **tomatillos**, preferably the milpero variety, husked and rinsed
2½ **cloves garlic**
¼ cup minced **white onion** (2¾ ounces/75 g)
3 **chiles de árbol**
3 **dried morita chiles**, stems removed
1 **guajillo chile**, stems and seeds removed
1 teaspoon **sea salt**, plus more if needed
1 tablespoon **orange juice**, freshly squeezed if in season

In a large saucepan over medium heat, bring the tomatillos, 2 garlic cloves, and the onion to a boil.

In the meantime, in a large cast-iron skillet over medium heat, toast the chiles, pressing down on them with a spatula for about 1 to 2 minutes each. The árbol chiles are the quickest to toast. When the moritas fluff up and the guajillo; when they change color slightly, they are done. Once toasted, add all the chiles to the pot of boiling water containing the tomatillos, garlic, and onion. Remove the saucepan from the heat. Allow the chiles to rehydrate for about 15 to 20 minutes with the rest of the ingrendients.

After the chiles have softened, drain the ingredients, discarding the soaking water. Remove and discard the stems and seeds of the moritas.

In a molcajete, add the salt, 2 cooked garlic cloves, and the remaining ½ clove raw garlic and grind using the pestle until the garlic has dissolved into a paste. Next, add the onion and do the same. Add one chile at a time and continue to grind until you are left with a paste. Lastly, add the cooled tomatillos, one by one, along with the orange juice. Smash with the pestle until the tomatillos have dissolved; it's OK if a few chunks remain. Taste and add more salt as needed.

Stir the salsa with a spoon and serve within 6 hours.

Salsa de Piña Tatemada

Makes 2 cups (480 ml)

There are some of us out there who are pineapple obsessed. We are the proud few who ask for extra piña in our taco de al pastor. We proudly order pineapple on pizza. We love Dole Whips and other sweet treats that contain pineapple. This salsa, dear piña lover, is for you. Don't forget that pineapple's special compound—bromelain—is good for meat digestion.

3 **cloves garlic**, peeled
1 large **red onion** (10½ ounces/300 g), minced
1 medium **pineapple**, peeled, cored, and cut into
  ¾-inch-thick (2 cm) slices
2 **habanero chiles**, stems removed
2 tablespoons **fresh lime juice**
1 teaspoon **sea salt**, plus more as needed
¼ cup (60 ml) **olive oil**
½ cup (25 g) minced **fresh flat-leaf parsley**

Start a charcoal or gas grill. Gas should be set to high. If using a pellet grill, preheat your grill to 425°F (220°C) for at least 15 minutes. If using charcoal, the coals should be red but entirely covered with gray ash.

Wrap the garlic and red onion in separate aluminum foil packets. Place them on the grill until the garlic and onion have softened, about 15 to 20 minutes.

Meanwhile, place the pineapple slices and habaneros directly on the grill. Cook until the pineapple has charred evenly on both sides and the skin of the habaneros has charred evenly, too, about 5 to 10 minutes. Turn every 2 to 4 minutes for even cooking. When charred, remove everything from the grill.

On a cutting board, chop the grilled pineapple into ¼ inch (6 mm) cubes. In a serving bowl, mix the pinapple with the grilled onion and the lime juice. Reserve.

Add the salt and garlic to a molcajete and grind until the garlic has dissolved into a paste. Next, slowly incorporate the habaneros and the olive oil, continuing to grind until you are left with a paste.

Add the habanero paste to the bowl of pineapple and onion, add the parley, and stir to combine. Taste for salt, adding more as needed, and serve.

Salsa Taquera Clásica

Makes 2 cups (480 ml)

This is a really nice, ubiquitous red salsa that everyone should have in their asada arsenal. You'll find versions of this salsa in every taquería and almost every supermarket deli section in the world, yet everyone has their own version of this delicious salsa.

2 tablespoons **grapeseed oil**
2 **guajillo chiles**, stems and seeds removed
15 **chiles de árbol**
1 **serrano chile**
2¾ cups (75 g) chopped **white onion**
2 **cloves garlic**, peeled
1 pound (455 g) **tomatillos**, preferably the milpero variety, husked and rinsed
1 teaspoon **sea salt**, plus more as needed

In a large frying pan over medium heat, add the oil. When hot, fry the chiles in batches, starting with the guajillos, cooking them until they change color and turning once so they don't burn, about 2 minutes. Remove to a plate.

Next, fry the chiles de árbol, stirring constantly until fragrant, about 2 minutes. Remove to a plate with the guajillos.

In the same oil, fry the serrano chile, onion, and garlic until the onions are translucent and a slight char has formed around the garlic and serrano, about 4 minutes. Remove from the heat and reserve on the plate.

Bring a large pot of water to a boil and add the tomatillos. Lower the heat and allow them to simmer until the tomatillos have changed color and cooked through, about 7 minutes. Using a slotted spoon, transfer the tomatillos to an ice bath to cool.

In a food processor or blender, add all of the chiles, the onion, garlic, tomatillos, and salt and blend until smooth.

Taste for salt, adding more as needed, and serve.

Salsa de Chile de Árbol y Morita Asada

Makes 2 cups (480 ml)

Certain dried chiles deliver varying levels of lingering heat. This salsa combines the zippy, instant heat of chiles de árbol with the deeper flavor and longer heat of moritas, making it one of the most well-rounded salsas you can make.

---

5 medium **roma tomatoes** (10½ ounces/300 g)
1 **serrano chile**, stem removed
2 tablespoons **grapeseed oil**
½ large **white onion** (6¼ ounces/175 g), sliced into thick rounds
2 **cloves garlic**, peeled
1 **dried morita chile**, stem and seeds removed
10 **chiles de árbol**
1 teaspoon **sea salt**

Start a charcoal or gas grill. Gas should be set to high. If using a pellet grill, preheat your grill to 425°F (220°C) for at least 15 minutes. If using charcoal, the coals should be red but entirely covered with gray ash.

Place the tomatoes and serrano directly on the grill and cook until they are softened and charred, about 10 to 15 minutes. Remove to a plate.

Heat the oil in a large frying pan over medium. When the oil is hot, fry the onion and garlic until they are translucent and a slight char has formed around the garlic, about 5 minutes. Add the morita chile and chiles de árbol. Stir for about 1 minute and remove from the heat.

In a food processor, add the tomatoes and serranos, the contents of the frying pan, and the salt, plus 2 tablespoons water. Blend, adding up to 2 tablespoons more if necessary, until smooth and serve.

Salsa Frita Verde

Makes 2 cups (480 ml)

If a salsa, rice, or birria consommé tastes inexplicably delicious, there is a high probability that it is made with a little bit of bouillon powder. It's usually "the secret ingredient" in dishes that cause you to ask yourself, *But why doesn't my version taste like that?* For this salsa, we lean all the way into chicken bouillon's MSG deliciousness. Set it out and see how many compliments you get at the carne asada. We bet it'll be a lot.

1 cup (240 ml) **olive oil**
6 **jalapeños** (5¼ ounces/150 g), sliced in half
2 **serrano chiles**, sliced in half
½ teaspoon **sea salt**
¼ cup (75 g) chopped **white onion**
3 **cloves garlic**, peeled
1 teaspoon **chicken bouillon powder**

Heat ½ cup (120 ml) of the olive oil in a large frying pan over medium heat. Add the jalapeños and serranos and stir until the chiles are fragrant and a slight char has formed around them, about 5 minutes. Stir in the salt and add the onion and garlic. Continue to cook for another 10 minutes, stirring occasionally, until the onions are translucent and a slight char has formed around the garlic. Remove from the heat.

Transfer the contents of the pan to a blender and add the bouillon powder. Blend until smooth and slowly incorporate the remaining ½ cup (120 ml) olive oil.

Pour the salsa into a bowl and serve at room temperature.

Salsa Roja Ranchera

Makes 2 cups (480 ml)

This is a versatile salsa that truly has it all: tomatillos, tomatoes, dried chiles, chopped onion for texture, and cinnamon. The cinnamon addition may sound weird at first, but it adds a flavor that immediately surprises guests at the first bite.

4 medium **roma tomatoes** (8½ ounces/240 g)

½ cup plus 2 tablespoons (100 g) minced **white onion**

10 **chiles de árbol**, stems and seeds removed

3 **guajillo chiles**, stems and seeds removed

6 **tomatillos**, preferably the milpero variety, husked and rinsed

2 **cloves garlic**, peeled and toasted in a dry skillet

1¼ inch (3 cm) **cinnamon stick**

¼ teaspoon **ground cumin**

1 teaspoon **sea salt**

½ teaspoon **dried oregano**

Bring a large pot of water to a boil and add the tomatoes, ½ cup (65 g) of the onions, and the chiles. After 5 minutes, add the tomatillos. Lower the heat and allow them to simmer until the tomatillos have changed color and cooked through, about 7 minutes. Using a slotted spoon, remove the tomatillos to a plate. Remove the tomatoes to a cutting board and remove their skins. Leave the chiles in the water until they are fully softened, about 10 more minutes.

Once the chiles are softened and the tomatillos have cooled, add them to a food processor or blender along with the cooked onion, garlic, cinnamon, cumin, and salt. Blend until smooth.

Serve immediately, topped with the 2 tablespoons reserved onion and the oregano.

Salsa de Morita Seca

Makes 2 cups (480 ml)

Chipotles are timeless, but I really love the heat that moritas offer. They are both made from jalapeños, but the difference is that moritas are smoked when the jalapeño is fully ripened and red, so it develops more heat. Using olive oil to bloom the chile really brings out its smoky qualities. It emulsifies and adds a nice mouthfeel to the salsa.

1 cup (240 ml) **olive oil**
6 **dried morita chiles**, stems removed
10 **chiles de árbol**
4 **cloves garlic** (12 g)
¼ teaspoon **ground cumin**
1 teaspoon **sea salt**, plus more as needed
2 tablespoons minced **fresh parsley**

Heat the oil in a large frying pan over medium heat. Fry the chiles in batches, starting first with the moritas, cooking them until they change color, turning once so they don't burn, about 2 to 3 minutes. Next, fry the chiles de árbol and garlic, constantly stirring until they are fragrant, about 2 to 3 minutes. Stir in the cumin in the last 30 seconds. Remove from the heat and let cool.

In a molcajete, grind the salt and garlic until the garlic has dissolved into a paste. Slowly incorporate the chiles and olive oil, continuing to grind until you are left with a paste. Stir in the parsley, taste, and season with more salt as needed.

A Better Pico

Makes 2 cups (480 ml)

People in Spain have been grating their tomatoes for pan con tomate for many generations. Same with Italians, to jumpstart their delicious long-cooked tomato sauces. We've applied the same technique to create a better pico; it is more like a paste and lends itself to being spooned on top of anything, from carne asada to eggs. The best part is that the salsa will stay in your taco and not all over your plate.

4 medium **roma tomatoes** (8½ ounces/240 g)
1 **clove garlic**, peeled
¼ cup (35 g) minced **white onion**
3 tablespoons finely chopped **fresh cilantro**
3 **jalapeños**, stemmed and finely chopped
¼ teaspoon **dried oregano**
¼ cup (60 ml) **fresh lime juice**
2 teaspoons **sea salt**

Using a cheese grater, grate the tomatoes one at a time over a bowl, preserving all their juices.

In a skillet over medium heat, toast the garlic until the edges are lightly charred. Mince.

In a bowl, combine the garlic with the onion, cilantro, jalapeños, oregano, lime juice, and salt. Serve immediately.

Salsa Tatemada en Molcajete

Makes 2 cups (480 ml)

When you think of salsa for a carne asada, chances are you think of this fire-roasted salsa. We like it extra spicy at our house, so we pack the chiles in. Chiles that are sitting in the refrigerator longer have a more stubborn spiciness to them with a heat that doesn't dissipate as quickly, so try to use the freshest chiles you can.

3 **cloves garlic**, peeled
4 medium **roma tomatoes** (8½ ounces/240 g)
8 **jalapeños** (7 ounces/200 g)
2 **serrano chiles**, if you like it extra spicy (optional)
1 teaspoon **sea salt**, plus more as needed

Start a charcoal or gas grill. The gas should be set to high. If using a pellet grill, preheat your grill to 450°F (230°C) for at least 15 minutes. If using charcoal, the coals should be red but entirely covered with gray ash.

Wrap the garlic in aluminum foil. Place the wrapped garlic, the tomatoes, and chiles directly on the grill and cook until they soften and are charred, about 5 to 10 minutes. Remove from the grill and set aside.

In a molcajete, grind the salt and garlic using the pestle until the garlic has dissolved into a paste. Next, slowly incorporate the chiles, continuing to grind until you are left with a paste. Add the tomatoes and continue to grind with the pestle until they are chunky. If needed, add 2 tablespoons water to thin the salsa and season with more salt.

Bone Marrow Salsa

Serves 8

This has to be the most decadent salsa ever created. It is inspired by a famous taco found in Monterrey, Mexico, made from juicy, thick Prime-grade arrachera steak cut into cubes and then topped with buttery roasted bone marrow. It is an extremely beefy salsa that takes carne asada into a beefy realm you never knew existed. However, it is also great on its own, spooned on a tortilla. Chiles güeros are medium-sized yellow chiles that aren't spicy but have an addicting bright flavor.

4 (5-inch/12 cm) **marrow bones**
4 medium **roma tomatoes** (8½ ounces/240 g)
4 fresh **chiles güeros** (3½ ounces/100 g), can be
    substituted with a fresh Anaheim green chile
½ large **white onion** (5½ ounces/150 g)
2 **cloves garlic**
1 tablespoon **sea salt**

Start a charcoal or gas grill. The gas should be set to high. If using a pellet grill, preheat your grill to 450°F (230°C) for at least 15 minutes. If using charcoal, the coals should be red but entirely covered with gray ash.

Place the marrow bones on the grill, marrow side up, along with the tomatoes, chiles güeros, and onion, cut side down. Close the cover.

Put the garlic in a molcajete. After 10 minutes, remove the tomatoes from the grill and place them in the molcajete. Mash into a chunky texture. Remove onions set aside.

After 30 minutes, remove the marrow bones. Let them cool slightly, then scoop out all the marrow into the salsa. Chop the onion and mash it with the rest of the salsa ingredients to incorporate. Serve warm.

Salsa Almendrada

Makes 2 cups (480 ml)

Sometimes, people forget that nut-based creamy salsas exist. However, a nuttier flavor can really complement and transform a variety of things. Spoon this over a quesadilla or tortilla topped with queso fresco and you'll see what I'm talking about. It goes well with vegetables as well.

¾ cup (6 ounces/180 ml) **olive oil**
3 **cloves garlic**, sliced
8 **cascabel chiles**, stems and seeds removed
4 **chiles de árbol**, stems and seeds removed
½ cup (80 g) **roasted almonds**
3 tablespoons **apple cider vinegar**
2 teaspoons **sea salt**

Add enough water to cover the chiles to a pot and bring to a boil over high heat.

Meanwhile, heat ½ cup (120 ml) of the oil in a large frying pan over medium heat. Add the garlic and fry until brown, stirring continually for about 4 minutes. Remove the garlic to a plate.

Add the chiles to the hot oil in batches, starting first with the cascabels, cooking and flattening them with a spatula until they change color, and turning once so they don't burn, about 2 to 3 minutes. Next, fry the chiles de arbol, stirring constantly until fragrant, about 2 to 3 minutes.

Remove the pan from the heat and, using tongs, submerge the chiles in the boiling water for about 20 minutes, until they have softened. Strain the chiles, reserving ¼ cup (60 ml) of the cooking water.

In a food processor or blender, add the softened chiles, fried garlic, the almonds, the remaining ¼ cup (60 ml) oil, the reserved soaking liquid, the vinegar, and the salt. Blend until smooth.

This salsa will stay fresh for up to 2 weeks in an airtight container in the refrigerator.

"Con Todo" Topping

Makes 2 cups (480 ml)

"Con todo" are the two magic words that you need to know when ordering tacos in L.A. or Mexico. It means that you're not afraid of the tacos staying with you long after eating them—in other words, you have no fear of biting into raw onion or having cilantro in your teeth. It indicates that you are a true lover of the taco life, which includes the sharp punch of raw onion. Some taquerías in L.A. have started to blend the cilantro and onion in one container so you can't have one without the other, just like in this topping.

1 large **white onion** (10½ ounces/300 g), minced
1 cup (40 g) **fresh chopped cilantro**, leaves and
    tender stems only
¼ cup (60 ml) **fresh lime juice**
½ teaspoon **sea salt**

In a medium bowl, stir together the onion, cilantro, lime juice, and salt until until evenly mixed. The salsa will keep, covered, in the refrigerator for up to 4 days.

Chamoy

Makes 2 cups (480 ml)

Chamoy is a thick, sour, and spicy fruit sauce possibly with Asian origins. It goes really well with sliced fruit, Mexican paletas, or sorbet, and can enhance beer or cocktails. It was originally made from salted or dried fruit. Somewhere along the way, it was watered down until most of the bottled stuff is not made from any fruit at all. This recipe is our ode to OG chamoy.

---

1 cup (50 g) **dried hibiscus blossoms**
1 cup (50 g) **dried apricots**
1 cup (50 g) **prunes**
1 cup (50 g) **unsweetened dried cranberries**
2 **chiles de árbol**, seeds and stems removed
½ cup (100 g) **sugar**
2 teaspoons **sea salt**
¼ cup (60 ml) **orange juice**, freshly squeezed if in season
¼ cup (60 ml) **fresh lime juice**

Pour 3 cups (720 ml) water into a medium stock-pot and add the hibiscus blossoms, apricots, prunes, cranberries, chiles, and sugar. Bring to a boil over medium-high heat. Once boiling, lower the heat to a simmer and cook for 20 minutes. Most of the water will be cooked off. Turn off the heat and let cool in the pot.

Once cool, transfer the cooked dried fruit mixture to a blender. Add the salt, orange juice, and lime juice. Blend until completely smooth, 1 to 2 minutes.

Pass the puree through a fine-mesh strainer and it's ready to serve. It will also stay good for up to 2 months stored in an airtight container in the refrigerator.

Chiles Toreados

Serves 4

Chiles toreados are chile peppers that are blistered and fried or grilled in a little hot oil. The dish gets its name from the action of rolling the chiles tightly in between your hand and a hard surface, which effectively makes them hotter by spreading the capsaicin around within the chiles. Like many deceivingly simple dishes, the secret is all about the quality of ingredients you use to make them. We use peanut oil because it is naturally nutty and aromatic.

3 tablespoons **peanut oil**
10 **serrano chiles** (3½ ounces/100 g), stems removed
4 wedges **lime**, for squeezing
Sea salt

Heat the oil in a medium pan over high heat. Once the pan is hot, add the chiles and fry them for about 10 minutes. Make sure to move them around so that all sides of the chiles get blistered and brown.

Once the chiles are browned, remove them to a plate. Squeeze fresh lime juice over them and sprinkle with salt to taste. Serve warm.

One thing that never should be missing from an asada are plenty of beverages. Bringing a case of cold beer is practically the price of admission to a carne asada, and sometimes that's all you need. But if you like to mix it up and have a few options for your guests who don't do beer, batched cocktails are the way to go; you can prepare them before the party and enjoy without having to constantly be shaking cocktails. Here are some of our favorites that we love to serve at our asadas, along with some chill aguas frescas.

LASAGUAS

Watermelon and Lime Zest Agua Fresca

Serves 12

We are all so used to squeezing lime juice into things, especially agua fresca, but often throw away the zest that can add another layer of citrusy intensity to things. I've learned to try using the zest where I would normally use lime juice, and the result, like in this agua de sandia, is usually amazing.

6 cups (900 g) cubed **seedless watermelon**
8 cups (2 L) **filtered water**
½ cup (100 g) **sugar**
Zest of 2 **limes**
1 tablespoon **fresh lime juice**
Pinch **sea salt**

In a high-speed blender, add the watermelon and 5 cups (1.2 L) of the water and blend until completely smooth.

Set a fine-mesh strainer over a pitcher and strain the mixture, pushing gently on the solids to extract as much liquid as possible.

In the same blender, add the remaining 3 cups (720 ml) water, the sugar, and lime zest. Blend until the sugar is completely dissolved.

Add the sugared water, lime juice, and salt to the pitcher and stir well to combine.

Chill the agua fresca for at least 3 hours. Serve over ice.

Mandarin and Mango Agua Fresca

Serves 6

Blending fresh mandarins into an agua fresca is a secret weapon against even the hottest of days. It is incredibly refreshing. Adding mango gives it a tropical vibe and makes the agua nectar-like.

1 cup (165 g) fresh or frozen and thawed **mango** chunks
1 cup (190 g) fresh or canned and well-drained **mandarin orange slices**
Juice of 1 **lime** (about 2 tablespoons)
5 cups (1.2 L) **filtered water**
½ cup (100 g) **sugar**

In a high-speed blender, add the mango, mandarins, lime juice, and 3 cups (720 ml) of the water and blend until completely smooth.

Set a fine-mesh strainer over a pitcher and strain the mixture, pushing gently on the solids to extract as much liquid as possible.

In the same blender, add the remaining 2 cups (480 ml) water and the sugar. Blend until the sugar is completely dissolved.

Pour the sugared water into the pitcher and stir well to combine.

Chill the agua fresca for at least 3 hours. Serve over ice.

Cantaloupe and Piloncillo Agua Fresca

Serves 10

Ripe cantaloupe, when in season, is one of the best fruits on the planet. The texture is so juicy and satisfying, and the flavor is somewhere between honey and vanilla. This agua fresca with piloncillo—unrefined brown sugar that is usually sold in a cone-shaped block—brings out cantaloupe's naturally sweet and floral flavors even more.

6 cups (950 g) cubed **cantaloupe**, seeds removed
5 cups (1.2 L) **filtered water**
1 cup (240 ml) canned **evaporated coconut milk**
4 ounces (115 g) **piloncillo**, grated
¼ teaspoon **ground cinnamon**

In a high-speed blender, add 5 cups of the cantaloupe and 4 cups (1 L) of the water and blend until completely smooth. Reserve last cup of cubed melon.

Set a fine-mesh strainer over a pitcher and strain the mixture, pushing gently on the solids to extract as much liquid as possible. Reserve the liquid and discard the solids.

In the same blender, add the remaining 1 cup (240 ml) water, the evaporated coconut milk, piloncillo, and cinnamon. Blend until the sugar is completely dissolved.

Pour the sweetened coconut milk into the pitcher with the cantaloupe water, add the reserved chopped bits of cantaloupe, and stir well to combine.

Chill the agua fresca for at least 3 hours. Serve over ice.

Orange, Pineapple, and Lime Agua Fresca

Serves 6

Agua de naranja is found all over Mexico. It's like the OG version of Tang! We add pineapple and lime to keep the vibes strictly tropical.

1 cup (240 ml) **fresh orange juice**
1 cup (165 g) **fresh pineapple chunks**
½ cup (120 ml) **fresh lime juice**
5 cups (1.2 L) **filtered water**
½ cup (100 g) **sugar**
1 **orange**, peeled, sliced, and chopped

In a high-speed blender, add the orange juice, pineapple chunks, lime juice, and 2 cups (480 ml) of the water and blend until completely smooth.

Set a fine-mesh strainer over a pitcher and strain the mixture, pushing gently on the solids to extract as much liquid as possible.

In the same blender, add the remaining 3 cups (720 ml) water and the sugar. Blend until the sugar is completely dissolved.

Add the sugared water and the chopped oranges to the pitcher and stir well to combine.

Chill the agua fresca for at least 3 hours. Serve over ice.

Lemongrass and Coconut Iced Herbal Tea

Makes 6 cups (1.4 L)

Straight up: This iced tea tastes like being on vacation. Every once in a while, I'll escape out to Punta Mita in Nayarit to relax with my husband. One time, a hotel welcomed me with a similar iced tea and it tasted so good in the hot tropical weather. This tea is inspired by that refreshing combination of lemongrass and coconut.

2 cups (200 g) **fresh coconut** chunks, peeled
6 cups (1.4 L) **filtered water**
1 **lemongrass** stalk
½ cup (100 g) **sugar**
Pinch **sea salt**

In a medium saucepan over high heat, combine the coconut with the water and bring to a boil. Reduce the heat to an active simmer, about medium-low, and let the coconut cook for 10 minutes. Cover and remove the pan from the heat.

On a cutting board, trim off the long, dry stalks from the lemongrass plus the root end, leaving the thicker bulb intact. (On most stalks this will be about 6 to 8 inches [15 to 20 cm] long.) Using a rolling pin, kitchen mallet, or the broad side of a cleaver, smash the bulb once or twice so that the insides are exposed but the bulb is still more or less in one piece. Add the smashed lemongrass to the saucepan and let the mixture steep, covered, for 30 minutes.

Remove the lemongrass bulb from the pan. Working in batches, transfer the coconut and steeping liquid to a high-speed blender and blend for 1 to 2 minutes, until very smooth.

Set a fine-mesh strainer over a pitcher and strain the mixture, pressing gently on the coconut solids to extract as much liquid as possible. Add the sugar and salt and stir until dissolved.

Chill the tea for at least 3 hours. Serve over ice.

Lemony Horchata con Manzanilla

Serves 6

In Mexico, its common to drink some *té de manzanilla* (chamomile tea) for its relaxing properties and also to settle your stomach. Adding dried chamomile flowers to horchata brings a unique floral sweetness to it.

1 **lemon**, peel scrubbed
1½ cups (285 g) **long-grain white rice**
4 cups (960 ml) **filtered water**
¼ cup (50 g) food-safe **dried chamomile flowers**
1½ cups (360 ml) **oat milk**
½ cup (100 g) **sugar**
Pinch of **sea salt**
Lemon peel twists, for garnish (optional)

Using a vegetable peeler, shave just the top layer of the bright yellow lemon peel into strips, working with light pressure to avoid the bitter white pith underneath.

In a high-speed blender, add the lemon peel, rice, and 2 cups (480 ml) water and pulse a few times to break up the grains. Add another 2 cups (480 ml) water and blend for about 1 minute, until the lemon peel is reduced to specks and the rice grains are quite small, but the mixture is not completely smooth. (Leaving some texture in the grains will help keep the end result from being overly starchy.)

Transfer the grain mixture to a large bowl, add the chamomile flowers, cover, and let sit at room temperature for at least 6 hours, ideally overnight.

Set a fine-mesh strainer over a pitcher and strain the mixture, pressing gently on the solids to extract as much liquid as possible. Add the oat milk, sugar, and salt and stir until the sugar is dissolved. Chill the horchata for at least 3 hours. Serve over ice with lemon peel twists for garnish, if you like.

Pictured here: The mixture before getting strained

Toasted Corn Horchata

Serves 6

No beverage goes better with grilled meat, tortillas, and salsa than sweet and cinnamony horchata. Don't ask us how or why; the combination just works. In this variation, the flavor and smell of toasted field corn (the kind of non-sweet dried corn that is used to make tortillas) have to be one of the best things in the world. When blended with rice, the toasted corn adds another layer of milky and refreshing goodness.

¾ cup (100 g) **white field corn kernels**
2 3-inch **cinnamon sticks**
¾ cup (145 g) **long-grain white rice**
4 cups (960 ml) **filtered water**
1½ cups (360 ml) **oat milk**
½ cup (100 g) **sugar**
1 teaspoon **vanilla extract**
Pinch **sea salt**
Ground cinnamon, for garnish

Add the corn kernels and cinnamon sticks to a small, dry cast-iron or nonstick pan. Set the pan over medium-low heat and toast the corn and cinnamon, shaking the pan every few minutes, until the corn is golden in spots and the pan is fragrant, 10 to 12 minutes.

Transfer the toasted corn and cinnamon to a high-speed blender. Add the rice and 2 cups (480 ml) water and pulse a few times to break up the grains. Add another 2 cups (480 ml) water and blend for about 1 minute, until the grains and kernels are quite small but the mixture is not completely smooth. (Keeping some texture in the grains will help keep the end result from being overly starchy.)

Transfer the mixture to a large bowl, cover, and let sit at room temperature for at least 6 hours, ideally overnight.

Set a fine-mesh strainer over a pitcher and strain the corn kernel mixture, pressing gently on the solids to extract as much liquid as possible. Add the oat milk, sugar, vanilla, and salt and stir until the sugar is dissolved.

Chill the horchata for at least 3 hours. Serve over ice and sprinkle with ground cinnamon.

Pictured here: The mixture before getting strained

For the Cooler

Nothing will ever beat that first sip of an ice-cold beer when you arrive to a carne asada, but once you're done with that beer and want to move on to other refreshing libations, here is an arsenal to choose from. Make them in advance and pre-batch so that guests can pour themselves and you don't have to be shaking up a storm instead of hanging out at your own asada.

Simple Syrup

Makes about 1 cup (480 ml)

Having simple syrup handy comes in clutch when batching cocktails. This recipe easily lends itself to be multiplied by two or more.

1 cup (200 g) **sugar**
1 cup (240 ml) **filtered water**

Put the sugar and water in a blender. Blend on high until the sugar is completely dissolved. Allow the mixture to settle for a few minutes to get rid of air bubbles. Store in a tightly sealed container in the refrigerator. Keeps for up to 6 weeks.

Margarita Toreada

Serves 6 to 8

This spicy margarita is usually made with muddled jalapeño or jalapeño syrup, so we decided why not grill the fresh green chile first? The result is a cocktail that holds its own against all the tacos you will eat at the carne asada. We use serranos for their sharp flavor.

1 small **serrano chile**, stems removed and sliced
8 ounces (240 ml) **tequila blanco**
8 ounces (240 ml) **tequila reposado**
8 ounces (240 ml) **fresh lime juice**
8 ounces (240 ml) **Simple Syrup** (page 236)
Chile-lime salt, for rimming glasses

If your grill is on, grill the serrano chile over an open fire until charred on all sides. If not, char it in a cast-iron pan over medium heat.

In a pitcher, muddle the serrano. Add the tequilas, lime juice, and simple syrup and stir well to combine. Add 2 cups (480 ml) ice.

When ready to serve, rim a glass with chile-lime salt, fill with ice, and pour about 4 ounces per cup.

Morita Michelada

Makes enough for 6 micheladas

In Oaxaca, our micheladas don't have much or any tomato cocktail mix. We depend on chiles and Worcestershire sauce to add a boost of savory flavor to them. We love them so much that my restaurant launched a bottled line of michelada mix inspired by this recipe.

2 **dried morita chiles**

6 ounces (180 ml) **tomato juice**

4 ounces (120 ml) **orange juice**, preferably freshly squeezed

2 ounces (60 ml) **fresh lime juice**

1¼ tablespoons **sugar**

1 tablespoon **sea salt**

½ teaspoon **freshly ground black pepper**

3 tablespoons **Worcestershire sauce**

Chile-lime salt, for rimming glasses

Cold Mexican lager (can substitute lime- or grapefruit-flavored sparkling water for a nonalcoholic version)

Fill a small saucepan with enough water to cover the chiles and bring the water to a boil over high heat. Remove the pan from the heat. Add the chiles to the hot water and allow them to soften and get tender, about 20 minutes.

Remove the chiles from the water and allow them to cool to room temperature. Put the chiles in a blender and add the tomato juice, orange juice, lime juice, sugar, salt, pepper, and Worchestershire sauce. Blend everything until smooth, then strain through a fine-mesh sieve into a cup with a pouring spout.

Rim a cold beer glass with the chile-lime salt. Pour about 3 ounces (85 ml) of the michelada mix into a beer glass, add 12 ounces (350 ml) cold lager, and stir to combine. Serve cold.

Sparkling Mezcal Water

Serves 6 to 8

When you want to stay hydrated and refreshed, but still turn up, this cocktail is your jam. It is bubbly mezcal-spiked lemonade that goes really well with anything on the carne asada table.

12 ounces (360 ml) **single-origin espadín mezcal**
12 ounces (360 ml) **fresh lemon juice**, preferably from Meyer lemons
2 ounces (60 ml) **fresh lime juice**, preferably from key limes
6 ounces (180 ml) **Simple Syrup** (page 236)
¼ teaspoon **sea salt**
6 cups (1.4 L) **sparkling water**
Bitters

In a pitcher, combine the mezcal, lemon and lime juices, syrup, and salt. Stir well to combine. Add the sparkling water and 2 cups (480 ml) thick ice.

When ready to serve, fill 6 to 8 glasses with the desired amount of ice. Divide the mezcal mixture evenly among the glasses and top each glass with a dash of bitters.

Tequila Colada

Serves 6 to 8

Piña coladas instantly get you in the mood to relax, unwind, and have a good time. This is our Mexified version of the iconic cocktail in which we use dark tequilas aged in oak barrels instead of rum. The standard for all colada beverages is Coco Lopez brand sweetened coconut milk, but if you prefer a less sweet cocktail, you can use evaporated coconut milk, which is sold online or at supermarkets like Whole Foods and Sprouts Farmers Market.

1 **lime**, scrubbed
6 ounces (180 ml) **sweetened cream of coconut**
6 ounces (180 ml) **tequila reposado**
4 ounces (120 ml) **fresh lime juice**
2 ounces (60 ml) **tequila añejo**

Using a vegetable peeler, shave the top green layer of the lime peel into strips, working with light pressure to avoid the bitter white pith underneath.

In a high-speed blender, add the lime peel, cream of coconut, reposado tequila, lime juice, and añejo tequila, and top with 4 cups (about 1 L) ice. Blend for 1 to 2 minutes, until the lime peel is reduced to flecks and the mixture is smooth.

Divide the cocktail among 6 to 8 cups and serve immediately.

Smoky Margarita de Jamaica

Serves 6

Blood orange gives this cocktail an even deeper red color and a raspberry-like sweetness. But you can take your pick between blood orange or lime, depending on your flavor preferences or what is available. If you've already got the grill going and want to be extra, you can briefly char the citrus halves, for about 15 to 30 seconds, before juicing them. This gets the juices going and makes it easier to squeeze. Plus, it adds a layer of smoky goodness, but it's not at all necessary.

For the toasted Jamaica syrup:
½ cup (25 g) **dried hibicus flowers (flor de Jamaica)**
1 cup (200 g) **sugar**

For the margaritas:
10 ounces (300 ml) **single-origin espadín mezcal**
10 ounces (300 ml) **fresh blood orange** or **lime juice**

For the garnishes:
Pink Himalayan sea salt
Chile-lime salt
Blood orange or **lime** wedges, for serving

Make the toasted hibiscus syrup: Add the hibiscus flowers to a small saucepan and set the pan over medium-low heat. Toast the dried flowers, shaking the pan occasionally, until they're faintly fragrant and a bit smoky, about 10 minutes. Add 1 cup (240 ml) water plus the sugar and increase the heat to medium-high. Bring the mixture to a boil and cook, stirring occasionally, for 5 minutes, until the sugar dissolves and the flowers soften.

Set a small strainer over a clean pint jar and carefully strain the syrup, pressing gently on the hibiscus flowers to extract as much liquid as possible. Let the syrup cool completely before using.

Make the margaritas: In a pitcher, add the mezcal, juice, and 1¼ cups (300 ml) of the hibiscus syrup and stir well to combine. Chill for at least 3 hours.

When ready to serve, on a small plate, combine a few tablespoons of pink salt and a few tablespoons of chile-lime salt. Run a blood orange or lime wedge around the rim of a glass and dip the rim in the chile-lime salt mixture to coat it.

Add a few ice cubes to the glass and pour the chilled margarita mixture over the ice. Garnish with the blood orange or lime wedge and serve.

Frozen Watermelon Mezcal Juice

Serves 4 to 6

Juicy and floral ripe watermelon goes so well with mezcal. This cocktail is dangerous because it is so easy to drink.

4 cups (600 g) cubed **seedless watermelon**
3 ounces (90 ml) **fresh lime juice**
3 ounces (90 ml) **Simple Syrup** (page 236)
8 ounces (240 ml) **single-origin espadín mezcal**
Sea salt, for finishing

In a high-speed blender, blend the watermelon chunks until they liquefy.

Set a fine-mesh strainer over a pitcher and strain the watermelon mixture, pressing gently on the solids to extract as much liquid as possible. Reserve the pulp and freeze it into ice cubes.

Mix the watermelon water with the lime juice, simple syrup, and mezcal. Stir to combine. Refrigerate while the ice cubes freeze.

When ready to serve, fill 4 to 6 9-ounce glasses with the frozen watermelon ice. Divide the mezcal mixture evenly among the glasses and top each serving with the finishing salt.

244

Sangrita

Serves 8 to 10

Sangrita is the original tequila chaser, and it tastes great while sipping on mezcal as well, especially the ones that are a little higher proof and let their agave qualities be known as they are going down the hatch. Making sangrita from scratch is a lost art but actually not that hard. It keeps for a while and adds an elegant and traditional vibe when drinking liquor straight.

12 ounces (360 ml) **tomato juice**
4 ounces (120 ml) **orange juice**, preferably
   freshly squeezed
2½ ounces (75 ml) **Simple Syrup** (page 236)
2 ounces (60 ml) **fresh lime juice**
3 tablespoons **I Love Michelada mix**
2 tablespoons **Tapatío hot sauce**
1 tablespoon **Tabasco sauce**
Chile-lime salt, for rimming shot glasses

In a large cocktail shaker, add the tomato juice, orange juice, simple syrup, lime juice, michelada mix, and the hot sauces. Shake to combine and store in the fridge. Keeps really well for up to 1 week. Serve in a shot glass rimmed with chile-lime salt next to your favorite mezcal or tequila.

Smoky Paloma

Serves 6 to 8

If you only served one batched cocktail at a carne asada, this one would be a strong contender. It's just the thing if you are a person who doesn't like your cocktails too sweet and instead prefers a little bit of bitterness in your life.

16 ounces (480 ml) **grapefruit juice**, preferably freshly squeezed
4 ounces (120 ml) **fresh lime juice**
2 ounces (60 ml) **Simple Syrup** (page 236)
8 ounces (240 ml) **tequila blanco**
8 ounces (240 ml) **single-origin espadín mezcal**
Chile-lime salt, for rimming glasses
16 ounces (480 ml) **grapefruit-flavored sparkling water** or **grapefruit soda**
1 **grapefruit**, peeled and sliced into thin wedges, for garnish

In a pitcher, combine the grapefruit juice, lime juice, simple syrup, tequila, and mezcal. Stir well to combine.

When ready to serve, rim a glass with chile-lime salt, fill with ice, and pour about 4 ounces per cup.

Carajillo

Makes 4

Originally from Spain, the carajillo is Mexico's official after-dinner drink. No matter where you are eating around the country, you will see people sipping this foamy, refreshing coffee-based cocktail to keep the vibe going and help them digest the meal they just enjoyed. The unsubstitutable Licor 43 this coffee cocktail depends on acts like a syrup that emulsifies when shaken with the coffee and ice, making this drink very dessert like.

8 tablespoons (40 g) **freshly ground coffee**
1 quart (1 L) **hot filtered water**
8 ounces (240 ml) **Licor 43**
Cacao nibs, for garnish

Put the coffee grounds in a French press and pour the hot water over. Allow to steep for 10 minutes.

When ready to serve, combine the coffee and the Licor 43 in an extra-large cocktail shaker and shake vigorously with ice until foamy. Fill four glasses with the desired amount of ice and strain the carajillo into each one of them. Sprinkle with cacao nibs to serve.

Something Sweet

Eating piles of juicy grilled meat has a way of making you crave something sweet at the end of it all. Carne asadas are never about dessert, but if you're lucky, you'll get a slice of birthday cake and maybe another fat slice to take home, too. If you want to go all out at your carne asada and serve dessert, too, here are some unfussy ways to end a day of feasting.

ALGO
DULCE

254

Bionico

Serves 6

Bionicos are Mexico's answer to fruit parfaits or fruit salads. Its roots are in Guadalajara, Jalisco, where it was created in the nineties, but it quickly became adopted all over the country for its healthy-ish qualities. You'll usually find bionicos served at juice shops. Obviously a bionico makes a solid breakfast, but since it is made with super velvety Mexican crema, it is rich enough to enjoy as a dessert as well. Feel free to make a bionico with any fruit you have on hand, including peaches and mangoes if you're making it in the summer.

2 cups (480 ml) **Mexican crema**

3 tablespoons **sugar**

1 tablespoon **vanilla extract**

1 cup (85 g) **unsweetened coconut shavings**

1 cup (165 g) sliced **strawberries**

1 cup (150 g) sliced **bananas**

1 cup (175 g) ripe cubed **cantaloupe**

1 cup (150 g) ripe cubed **papaya**

1 cup (180 g) diced **Pink Lady apples** or other crisp, slighlty tart apples

1 cup (150 g) **granola with raisins**

In a bowl, whisk together the crema, sugar, and vanilla extract to combine.

In a medium pan over low heat, lightly toast the coconut shavings until they are aromatic and the edges start to brown, about 3 minutes.

In a large serving bowl, gently toss together the strawberries, bananas, cantaloupe, papaya, and apples. Top with the vanilla crema, toasted coconut, and granola and serve.

Gelatina de Mosáico

Makes 10

Mexican gelatin desserts are overdue for a comeback. They are absolutely perfect as a last-minute dessert at a carne asada since they come together with just a handful of pantry ingredients. Gelatinas de mosáico also look absolutely stunning, making them a no-fuss way to celebrate a birthday or other special occasion. It is also a suprisingly light dessert after a heavy meal.

¼ cup (30 g) **unflavored gelatin powder**
¾ cup (180 ml) **warm water**
1 cup (240 ml) **whole milk**
1 cup (240 ml) **sweetened condensed milk**
1 cup (240 ml) **evaporated milk**
1 cup (240 ml) **Mexican sour cream**
1 tablespoon **vanilla extract**
1 (3-ounce/85 g) box **natural cherry gelatin mix**
1 (3-ounce/85 g) box **natural orange gelatin mix**
1 (3-ounce/85 g) box **natural lime gelatin mix**
1 (3-ounce/85 g) box **natural blueberry gelatin mix**

In a medium bowl, sprinkle the gelatin powder over the warm water. Whisk until it starts to dissolve. This should take about 10 minutes.

Prepare the cherry, orange, lime, and blueberry gelatins according to package directions. Pour each flavor into its own gelatin mold greased with coconut oil spray. Once they start to cool to room temperature, place all of the gelatin molds into the freezer for about 30 minutes so they can set. If you don't have space in the freezer for this, you can allow them to set in the refrigerator, but note that this will take longer about 1½ hours.

In another medium bowl, add the whole milk, sweetened condensed milk, evaporated milk, Mexican sour cream, and vanilla extract. Whisk until all the ingredients are evenly mixed. Add the dissolved gelatin powder mixture and continue whisking until it is fully combined. Set aside.

Once the flavored gelatins are set, remove them from the refrigerator or freezer. Flip them over onto a cutting board to unmold and cut the gelatin into 2-inch (5 cm) cubes.

Working in three batches, add the milk gelatin and spread it out evenly into a 9 by 3-inch (23 by 7.5 cm) well-greased Bundt pan (we recommend using a pan with a nice decorative pattern) with a rubber spatula. Add a layer of flavored gelatin cubes. Repeat two more times until the mold is full and the flavored gelatin is evenly distributed.

Put back into the fridge for 3 hours or until the dessert is all set. Slice and serve.

Paletas de Naranja con Chamoy

Makes 12 paletas

Come the hot weather, chamoy on everything is pretty much how we roll in our household. We drizzle this sweet and sour sauce on sliced mangoes, on micheladas, and use it in these orange paletas—Mexican ice pops—that work great as a palate cleanser after a meal.

3 cups (720 ml) **filtered water**
½ cup (100 g) **sugar**
1 cup (240 ml) **freshly squeezed orange juice**
¼ cup (60 ml) **fresh lemon juice**
2 **oranges**, peeled, sliced, and finely chopped
¾ cup (180 ml) **chamoy** (preferably homemade; recipe on page 213)
Chile powder or **sea salt**, for garnish

Blend the water and sugar in a blender until the sugar has completely dissolved. Mix in the orange juice, lemon juice, and chopped orange bits.

Pour the orange base into popsicle molds. Freeze overnight.

The next day, remove the popsicles from their molds, one at a time, and set aside on a plate. Add about 1 tablespoon chamoy to the bottom of each mold and return the frozen paletas to the molds. Return to the freezer and freeze for at least 1 hour.

You can sprinkle the tops with your favorite chile powder or salt before serving!

Jamaica, Ginger, and Blackberry Paletas

Makes 12 paletas

Having homemade paletas at your carne asada is extra, but all the kids running around willl love you forever for it. Jamaica blossoms are great in agua fresca but even more refreshing in paleta form.

¾ ounce (20 g) **dried hibiscus flowers** (flor de Jamaica)
1¼-inch (3 cm) piece **cinnamon stick**
1-inch (2.5 cm piece **fresh ginger**, peeled
4 cups (1 L) **filtered water**
½ cup (50 g) **sugar**
2 pints (560 g) **fresh blackberries**

In a 2-quart (2 L) saucepan over medium heat, bring the hibiscus flowers, 1½ cups (360 ml) water, the cinnamon, and ginger to a simmer. Cover and simmer for 15 minutes.

Remove from the heat and allow the mixture to steep for 10 minutes. Pass through a fine-mesh strainer and into a pitcher along with the 4 cups (960 ml) filtered water. When straining, apply pressure to the hibiscus leaves so you get every last little bit of juice. While the liquid is still lukewarm, add the sugar and mix well until mostly dissolved. Let cool.

Mash the blackberries until they form a paste. Pour 2 teaspoons blackberry paste into each popsicle mold, add the Jamaica concentrate, and freeze overnight before unmolding and serving.

Chocolate de Agua Paletas

Makes 12 paletas

Drinking chocolate in Oaxaca is never made with milk; it is made with water. When frozen into a paleta, it is like a chocolate sorbet. The naturally occurring cacao butter in Mexican chocolate makes the popsicles surprisingly creamy, despite the chocolate not having added emulsifiers and cacao butter that European chocolate has.

5¼ ounces (150 g) **Mexican chocolate**, chopped (about three round tablets)
¼ cup (50 g) **sugar**
¼ teaspoon **vanilla extract**

In a large saucepan, bring 4 cups (1 L) water to a boil. Right before it boils, add the chopped chocolate tablets, sugar, and vanilla extract. Using a molinillo or whisk, mash the chocolate as best you can until it dissolves and then whisk it until frothy. Remove from the heat and let cool.

Pour into popsicle molds and freeze overnight before unmolding and serving.

Churros Borrachos

Serves 12

Yes, this recipe translates to "drunken churros." Making churros at home from scratch is a game changer, especially if you've only had the pre-made ones usually found in theaters and amusement parks that tend to be on the dry side. Fresh churros are golden brown and crispy on the outside with custardy dough on the inside. Adding beer to the dough follows the same principle of a beer batter; the carbonation makes the batter light while adding a nice malty flavor.

8 ounces (240 ml) **dark Mexican beer**

3 tablespoons **salted butter**

2 tablespoons **crushed piloncillo** (can be substituted with dark brown sugar)

½ teaspoon **salt**

1 cup (125 g) **all-purpose flour**

1 large **egg**

1 teaspoon **vanilla extract**

¼ cup (50 g) **sugar**

2 teaspoons **ground cinnamon**

2 cups (480 ml) **peanut oil**

In a medium saucepan, combine the beer, butter, piloncillo, and salt. Bring to a boil over medium heat. Add the flour all at once, stirring with a spoon. Cook and stir until the mixture forms a ball and pulls away from the sides of the pan. Remove from the heat and let cool for 10 minutes. Mix in the egg and vanilla, beating well with a rubber spatula.

Transfer the batter to a piping bag fitted with a large star tip. (If you don't have a piping bag, clip one corner off a gallon-size zip-tight bag, and you can squeeze the batter through there.) Place in the refrigerator while you heat the oil for deep-frying. Mix together the sugar and cinnamon on a plate. Set aside.

In a deep saucepan, heat the peanut oil to between 350°F and 375°F (175°C and 190°C). Remove the piping bag from the refrigerator and slowly squeeze 3-inch (7.5 cm) strips of batter into the hot oil. Fry in batches, until the churros are golden brown, 5 to 6 minutes, flipping halfway through. Drain on a plate lined with paper towels.

Roll the warm churros in the cinnamon-sugar mixture to coat. Serve churros while still warm.

Grilled Plantains con Piña and Rompope

Serves 4

This is an asada version of a famous dessert widely sold along the city streets of Mexico and Los Angeles. To add an extra layer of tropical flavor, the plantains and pineapple are grilled on top of the pineapple peel. Instead of the usual sweetened and condensed milk, we finish this dessert with a drizzle of rompope, which is like a Mexican eggnog, to add some thick and rich boozy vanilla goodness.

1 medium **pineapple**
4 **ripe plantains** (2½ pounds/1.2 kg), peeled
Rompope, for serving
¼ cup (30 g) **pecans**, toasted and chopped

Preheat your grill to 375°F (190°C) if using a pellet grill, to low heat if using gas, or for indirect cooking if using charcoal, with the lid closed, for 15 minutes.

Using a chef's knife, slice the peel off the pineapple into large sheets, reserving the peels. Slice the rest of the pineapple vertically into ½-inch (12 mm) slices and remove the fibrous core.

Place the large sheets of pineapple peel on the grill, and then place the plantains on top. Layer the pineapple spears over the plantains. Cover and grill for 30 to 40 minutes, until the plantains are tender.

After another 15 minutes, the plantains should be deeply yellow and slightly caramelized. Remove the plantains and pineapple spears from the grill and arrange them on a plate. (Discard the grilled pineapple peels.) Drizzle with rompope and top with the toasted pecans.

Bricia Lopez

is an entrepreneur, cultural ambassador, and key figure in the Los Angeles gastronomic scene. With her family's James Beard Award–winning restaurant, Guelaguetza, in Los Angeles's Koreatown, she and her siblings have put Oaxacan cuisine and culture at the forefront of today's dynamic culinary scene. Her influence extends to the beverage industry, too. *The New Yorker* called Bricia the "queen of mezcal." In 2019, she helped open Las Vegas's first-ever mezcal bar—Mama Rabbit, inside the Park MGM. Her cookbook, *Oaxaca: Home Cooking from the Heart of Mexico*, published in fall 2019, was a 2020 James Beard nominee and became an Amazon bestseller with more than 750 five-star reviews.

Bricia and her siblings launched two direct-to-consumer brands: a proprietary michelada cocktail called I Love Micheladas™ and Guelaguetza™ mole pastes. Their products can also be found at hundreds of retailers across California. She has expanded her success into the digital world by launching the *Super Mamas* podcast with her sister Paulina and her blog *Mole and More*, where she shares simple recipes to cook at home with family. Bricia also holds lifestyle content creation partnerships with major brands.

The mayor of Los Angeles appointed Bricia to the board of convention and tourism development in March 2019, and in 2020 she cofounded RE:Her, a nonprofit devoted to the advancement and empowerment of women restaurateurs. She lives in Los Angeles with her husband Eduardo, son, and daughter and frequently travels to Oaxaca.

Javier Cabral

was born in East Hollywood and raised in the backyards of East L.A. and the San Gabriel Valley. At a young age he became obsessed with the things we eat and drink and, in 2006, started one of the first food blogs in Los Angeles, titled *Teenage Glutster*. Finding his passion for food and writing at an early age helped him stay focused and come out of the 'hood.

At sixteen, he published his first paid article about Mexican American holiday food traditions at the now-defunct magazine *LàTeen*. He proudly attended Pasadena City College, but after getting rejected by University of Southern California due to his poor grades in algebra, he dropped out of school to write about food full-time. He hasn't looked back. At twenty-one, working under James Oseland, he landed his first cover story about the rustic cuisine of Zacatecas, Mexico, for *Saveur*. Since then, he's become an authority on all things L.A., Mexican American culture in the U.S. and Mexico, tacos, and punk rock.

In 2012, he became an official restaurant scout for the late food critic Jonathan Gold. He proudly worked for the *Los Angeles Times* as the literal extension of Gold's belly. In 2016, he was hired as the West Coast editor and staff writer for *Vice MUNCHIES*, covering the California, Oregon, and Washington food and drink scenes for a national audience. His writing has been featured in over a dozen publications, including *Food & Wine*, *Lucky Peach*, the *Washington Post*, *Bon Appétit*, *Epicurious*, and *Razorcake*. At twenty-nine years old, he published his first anonymous starred restaurant review for the (old) *LA Weekly*.

His first cookbook, *Oaxaca: Home Cooking from the Heart of Mexico*, with Bricia Lopez, was published by Abrams Books in October 2019. He currently works as editor-in-chief of the independent local food, news, and culture site L.A. TACO, and associate producer for *The Taco Chronicles* on Netflix, both of which earned him coveted James Beard Award wins in 2020. He lives in Long Beach with his wife, Paola (who makes the best ceviche in the world), and his Old English sheepdogs, Fig and Crema.

Acknowledgments

I first thought about this book in the summer of 2020. I was nine months pregnant and, given the state of the world, it was the first summer I was not able to host friends and family to our celebratory asadas. My daughter came into my life on July 15. I was forced to slow down, be home, and enjoy this precious time that otherwise would have been cut short for me given the nature of my career, but I missed hosting tremendously. I missed having friends over. I missed the idea of people indulging over juicy meats, salsa, and crunchy chicharrones. Around the same time, my brother reached out, asking recipe questions for a Fourth of July feature photoshoot he was having at home for a national publication. I was home with a newborn and a five year old, so all I could do was live vicariously through my recipes and my brother.

They say that when a new life is born, she brings with her a new source of energy and blessings. My daughter was no different, because as soon as I saw the pictures from my brother's article, I knew I had a book in me to write.

I began researching books on carne asadas but nothing popped up. To my surprise, there was nothing dedicated to the art of Mexican-style grilling as it is done among Mexican immigrant households in the US. Sure, there are plenty of books out there that will include a recipe or two, but none dedicated to something as sacred and beautiful as a carne asada.

I called my book agent, Jonah, right away. He loved the idea and asked me to draft something up. Next, I called up Javi, my brother-from-another-mother and writing partner in all of this. Javi and I have always had an unspoken language when it comes to food, drink, and writing. He immediatetly understood what I wanted to write and achieve with this book. Without him, this book would not be the same.

Needless to say, a newborn, a five year old, and running a restaurant in the middle of a pandemic took priority. It took a whole other year for me to get my act together and put a proposal together for my editor, Holly. Holly has always been a champion for me at Abrams. She believed in me and what I hoped to accomplish with this book and provided me with all the tools and creative freedom I needed. Holly, thank you for understanding the importance of inclusion of women of color in the world of grilling. There are few of us, but the door you opened for me will soon be a gateway for many to follow.

After we got the greenlight from Abrams, I obsessed over this book. I lived and breathed the asada lifestyle 24/7. And it's at this point in the story where I have to acknowledge my life partner, husband, and best friend, Eduardo. My husband took charge with all home duties, including virtual schooling, and extra-curricular activities for the kids. He was there with me during late nights, picking up my kitchen mess and doing last minute runs to the grocery store. I am blessed to have him.

My siblings held down the fort at Guelaguetza. Paulina, thank you for being the badass boss that you are and looking out for me and everyone else. Guelaguetza would not be where it is today without your selfless leadership. Thank you for being the greatest sister a girl could ask for and for always believing in me even at times when I didn't. Fernando, you are a creative genius and everyone's favorite brother. *Asada* is as much your idea as it was mine. I could never do life without you. I love you both so much. We won't stop until the whole world hosts asadas at home with an I Love Micheladas bottle in their hand!

To my dad and mom who flew all the way from Oaxaca to help and be here for me during the book shoot and to my little sis for always being down and the first to all of my asadas. *Los amo!*

I want to thank my entire team at Guelaguetza, I Love Micheladas, and Super Mamas. Every single one of you shows up time after time for me and my family at times when we do passion projects like these and I am beyond grateful.

To the creative geniuses that took time out of their lives to help this book come to life, thank you for seeing my vision. Thank you to the greatest food photographer of all time and my honorary Oaxacan brother, Quentin Bacon. QB, I could never thank you enough or do another book without you. To Jesse Ramirez, for not only being a meticulous recipe tester and a great chef, but for also being patient with my mom jokes, constant unsolicited advice, and blasting Bad Bunny nonstop during our shoot days. To the greatest prop stylist, Nidia Cueva, who came to my rescue time after time again with my last minute calls and crazy ideas. Thank you *hermana*!

Thank you also to Alyssa Noui for the food styling and Janelle Hayner for the help in development.

This book was started from an idea prompted by a pandemic that affected millions of people across the globe. I am blessed to have the opportunity to bring a bit of joy and represent my culture through my cooking. I want to acknowledge those who had to say goodbye too soon to loved ones.

May this book light a fire in your heart.

Index

Page numbers in *italics* indicate photos.

Aguachile Rojo, *116*, 117
aguas. *See* beverages
alcohol. *See* beverages, with alcohol
Anaheim chiles, 14
apples, in Bionico, 255
Arrachera Verde, 74–*75*
Arroz Blanco, *144*, 145
Arroz Rojo, *140*, 141
Arroz Verde, 142–*43*
asada
    about: meaning of, 9
    historical overview, 12
    hosting and making carne asada, 11
    photo of spread, 10
    preparing for, 9–11
    true carne asada, 9
    what one looks like, 9–11
asparagus, in Grilled Veggies with Pipián Dip, 150–*51*
avocados
    Avocado Oil Flour Tortillas, 46–*47, 50*
    Blended Guacamole, 40–41
    Guacamole Tatemado en Molcajete, *42*, 43
    Salsa Asada de Aguacate, *188*, 189
    Salsa Verde con Aguacate, 190–*91*

bananas
    Bionico, 255
    Grilled Plantains con Piña and Rompope, 263
beans
    about: freshness and preparing, 136; herb helping in digestion of (*See* epazote)
    Frijoles Charros in Broth, 132–*33*
    Frijoles de la Olla, 136–*37*
    Frijoles Negros de la Olla con Nopalitos, *134*, 135

Editor: Holly Dolce
Managing Editor: Mike Richards
Designer: Jennifer Wagner
Design Manager: Danielle Youngsmith
Production Manager: Denise LaCongo

Library of Congress Control Number: 2022942325
ISBN: 978-1-4197-6288-8
eISBN: 978-1-64700-995-3
Text copyright © 2023 Bricia Lopez and Javier Cabral
Photographs copyright © 2023 Quentin Bacon
Cover © 2023 Abrams

Printed and bound in China

10 9 8 7 6 5 4 3 2 1

Abrams books are available at special discounts
when purchased in quantity for premiums and
promotions as well as fundraising or educational use.
Special editions can also be created to specification.
For details, contact specialsales@abramsbooks.com
or the address below.

Abrams® is a registered trademark of Harry N.
Abrams, Inc.

ABRAMS The Art of Books
195 Broadway, New York, NY 10007
abramsbooks.com